WAKEFIELD
Memories

Wakefield Cathedral Church of All Saints, c. 1890, before the building of the Walsham Howe extension and St Mark's Chapel. There has been a church on this site since the late tenth century. Parts of the eleventh-century Norman church are incorporated in the current building, which was built progressively from 1315, after the central tower collapsed and destroyed the nave and aisles. The current tower and spire were not built until the fifteenth century, and have dominated the Wakefield cityscape ever since.

WAKEFIELD
Memories

PAUL DAWSON

SUTTON PUBLISHING

First published in 2005 by
Sutton Publishing Limited · Phoenix Mill
Thrupp · Stroud · Gloucestershire · GL5 2BU

British Library Cataloguing in Publication Data
A catalogue record for this book is available from the British Library

ISBN 0-7509-3926-5

Typeset in 10.5/13pt Galliard and 10/13 Avant Garde
Typesetting and origination by
Sutton Publishing Limited.
Printed and bound in England by
J.H. Haynes & Co. Ltd, Sparkford.

Contents

Prologue

W hat are memories? Memories are a recollection of the past through written, oral and visual testimonies. The quotations in this book are all based on memories. The oral record is often more evocative than the written word as it can convey the feelings and personalities of those involved. The book is based on the oral testimonies of the people involved, both through recent interviews and historical accounts for newspapers. These are a valuable source of information for the local historian; it is possible to get more than one view of an event direct from people who witnessed it, rather than the established, abridged, version that appears in history books.

With this work, I aim to inform the present generation about aspects of Wakefield's history that have not been 'remembered' by previous authors and local history writers. By using personal testaments, diaries, letters and contemporary images, I hope to make the past a place of humanity: more accessible to the reader and not dealing merely with cold facts.

Acknowledgements

I would like to thank the following, without whose help this book would not have come to fruition, especially the Harvey clan (the late Ron Swinden JP, Mrs Shirley Murdock, Mr David Murdock, Mrs Jeane Cresswell, the late Eric Swinden, Mrs J. Simpson, Mr D. Varey, Mrs J. Dawson, Mr A.L. Dawson, the late Eric Bradley), as well as the late Mrs Gwen Simpson, Mr Colin Barker, Mr Dixon Holliday, Mrs D. Abson, Mr Keith Wainwright, Mrs R. Tetley, Mrs R. Haggis, St Austin's Church Wakefield, The BBC People's War, Mr B. Hartley, Mrs M. Walker, Mrs M. Firth and the staff of WMDC library services. All the photographs are from the author's collection apart from those of the cinemas (pp. 32, 47, 48) and Holy Trinity Church (p. 76), for which I am indebted to Ms Kate Taylor. I would also like to thank Miss Emily Hamilton for her continued support.

Paul L. Dawson BSc Hons, FINS, Wakefield, 2005

The Changing City

Wakefield is situated in the wool/textile belt of the former West Riding of Yorkshire, with the conurbations of Leeds to the north, Bradford to the west and the steel centre of Sheffield to its south. It came to national prominence in 1888 when it became a cathedral city and a year later when it became the county town for the West Riding of Yorkshire.

The city lies on the edge of the gravel terrace of the flood plain of River Calder and would have been an arid island surrounded by the sands and clays of the flood plain. The area would have been marshy ground *c.* 6000 BC. This has always been, and remains, a rich agricultural area. Neolithic (4000–2000 BC) settlements are known to have existed in Stanley and Wakefield, and Iron Age (700 BC–AD 43) farmers ploughed the south-facing slope of the town. The Romans (AD 43–410) built two roads through Wakefield – the current Westgate and Kirkgate/Northgate. For the Romans, Wakefield had many strategic advantages based on its good transportation networks. The Calder led to the Humber estuary and the North Sea, allowing supplies to be easily imported. The river also gave access to the valleys of the Pennines. The land routes gave access to the Pennines as well as to the fortress at York and the nearby fort at Castleford. For Wakefield, the archaeological and historical record is blank for 300 years once the Roman military had departed in AD 410. In AD 735 York became an archbishopric and St Paulinus built a church at Dewsbury. Wakefield received the teaching of Christ at this time and a cross was erected in the market place at the crossroads of the two Roman roads.

In AD 866 Yorkshire and Wakefield became part of the Norse Empire. The impact of the takeover is still apparent in Wakefield street names; for example those, like Westgate, which incorporate the old Norse word *gata*, which means street. In the eleventh century Wakefield was owned by the Saxon Kings of England and held as a Royal estate, although no trace of it can be found today.

When the Normans replaced the Saxon rulers of England in 1066, Wakefield became part of the estate of the Earl of Surrey, William Warrenne, who built castles at Sandal and Wakefield and also rebuilt the Saxon churches of Sandal, Horbury and Wakefield. Wakefield Castle was abandoned by 1300 in favour of Sandal. From 1450 onwards, Wakefield grew as an important wool centre; this new wealth is shown in the rebuilding of the parish church of All Saints and the lost church of St John the Baptist. The Reformation of religious practices of 1536–9 saw the closure of the four unique chantry chapels, St Mary the Virgin, St Mary Magdalene, St Swithin and St John the Baptist. Only St Mary the Virgin remains today: it can be seen standing on Wakefield's medieval bridge across the River Calder.

Bread Street, c. 1900. Bread Street was originally a number of medieval streets, which in-filled the medieval market place at the top of Westgate. The name refers to the main commodity available. In medieval times all bread and pies had to be baked at the manor bakehouse, which was situated on Mary Gate. The bakehouse was demolished to make way for the church institute in the middle of the nineteenth century.

After perhaps two centuries or so of growth, and after being interrupted by the Civil War, the restoration of the monarchy resulted in new town houses being built. By 1700, Wakefield entered a long and stable period of growth, becoming the county town of West Yorkshire by 1800. By the turn of the nineteenth century, Wakefield was considered to be the capital of the West Riding. The town was at the peak of a material prosperity based primarily on its wool trade with Russia. This success, which was built on the back of the Industrial Revolution, drew people into the town to work in the many mills and dye works. The collapse of the wool trade in 1820, the stock market in 1825, and the shift to the Gold Standard in the following year, brought ruin to many of the town's industrialists.

By the mid-nineteenth century, Wakefield had experienced a period of extensive change, influenced by industrialisation. It had evolved into a market town and service centre of some significance. The stagnation of the cloth industry and the depression of the 1820s heralded a period of gradual decline. The damaging effect this had on the local economy was paralleled in the activity of its citizens, its cultural and social life and its other institutions. It also saw a rapid growth in the working class. This led many to believe that the civilising power of the church was needed to ensure the working class did not lead godless lives.

The population of Wakefield grew by 53 per cent in the first half of the nineteenth century. Although this seems a large increase it was small in comparison to the 62–93 per cent experienced by neighbouring towns such as Leeds and Bradford. The increase placed pressure on Wakefield's housing stock, water supply and sewage disposal, as, unlike its neighbours, Wakefield did not undergo spatial expansion.

The failure of Wakefield to expand commercially in the nineteenth century has been blamed, by some commentators, on the dominance of a local and inert aristocracy. The town, from the middle of the eighteenth century, had become a much-sought-after residential town that attracted people who were unconnected with trade and contributed little to the economic activity and well being of the town. Indeed, in the 1851 census, 28 per cent of the population are recorded as contributing nothing to the economy of the town. The social structure of the town also contained a very active middle class, which consisted primarily of the merchant prince families of, among others, the Naylors, Milnes, Heywoods, Pembertons. These people, classed as professional persons, built large houses for themselves in new residential areas such as Saint John's and South Parade and became influential in the local politics of the day.

To say that, during the nineteenth century, Wakefield stagnated may be an exaggeration, although it did fail to capitalise on its natural advantages; it had a good transport and communication network of road, rail and canal, a plentiful supply of local coal, an established cloth manufacturing and marketing industry and perhaps the largest corn and cattle markets in Europe. Economic decline was offset by agriculture, rope manufacturing, brewing and malting and the chemical and soap industries. It would appear that the nineteenth century was a period of lost opportunities and lack of enterprise.

Northgate, c. 1900. Northgate was one of medieval Wakefield's four principal roads and, like Westgate, follows the line of a Roman road. At the head of Northgate, on the site of Queen Elizabeth Grammar School, was the church of St John the Baptist, which was demolished in the eighteenth century after being closed as a place of worship during the Reformation. Near to the church was Hazeldene Hall, a fine medieval and Tudor mansion, which was demolished in the 1950s. The site is partly occupied by Charlie Brown's garage.

Urban growth during the nineteenth century brought Wakefield's expanding population and industry into close proximity; the population grew from 12,232 in 1831 to 21,076 in 1871, with an average of five people per house. The apparent lack of religious belief (or at least its practice) among this working class and urban poor was a constant Victorian concern. These people had been drawn to the town in the early and mid-nineteenth century by the Industrial Revolution. Many in the 1830s and 1840s held the view that the absence from worship led to the growth of anti-establishment activities, in particular to Chartism and Methodism. These activities were in part an attempt to improve the lot of the working class: a not surprising undertaking given their living conditions. It was in these new industrial areas that the evangelical revival of the early nineteenth century took hold.

It is hardly surprising, therefore, that proposals to extend the influence of the church, reflected by a need to maintain a respectable and god-fearing public, emerged in the early 1840s. There were some districts, housing the families of the labouring classes, where the link with the established church had almost been sundered. This had enabled the nonconformists to infiltrate. New churches were proposed as a means of overcoming this threat.

Lord Ashley, campaigning in the House of Commons for extra funds for national schools, argued that the principles of religion and respectability should be taught in schools as a matter of urgency to counteract the 'terrible wilderness of spiritual devastation', which he linked to the upturn in crime and drunkenness.

All of this resulted in an enabling measure, the Church Extension Act of 1843, with the aim of making 'better provision for the spiritual care of populous parishes'. A year later, a specific act was passed by the Prime Minister of the day, Robert Peel authorising the creation of two new and neighbouring, largely working class, ecclesiastical districts and a new parish. The parish of Holy Trinity was established on 20 October 1844, and the districts of St Andrew's and St Mary's on 3 September 1844 in the south-eastern part of Wakefield.

However, Wakefield, like most parts of Yorkshire, was strongly nonconformist in its religious convictions. The strength of the Methodist movement is indicated by twenty-five Wesleyan Methodist and twenty-six Primitive Methodist preaching places in 1823, and only two Anglican churches. The foundations of these societies and their buildings were still in evidence in 1920: the strength of this movement was based upon the loyalty of individual families. The Education Act of the 1870s made basic education available to all, which resulted in far more people attaining literacy. This affected the order of service in both nonconformist and established churches. Nonconformist culture had a major impact on Wakefield in the nineteenth century, its heyday being 1880–1910. The church provided many with an opportunity to better themselves, through education and abstinence from vices, and, in an era before radio and television, in a place of entertainment that was designated as clean. By the 1880s, many, if not all, of the churches and chapels had their own choirs. This was primarily because a larger proportion of the congregations were literate and thus could take part in new church activities. This culture survived intact until the Second World War, and is vividly recalled by Ron Swinden and Gilbert Brummit later in the book.

Looking down Almshouse Lane towards George Street, c. 1900. Almshouse Lane, like South Gate and Cock & Swan Yard (later Bishop Gate), was a small lane, which ran between the long burgage plots of medieval Wakefield to the town boundary, near the current George Street. George Street used to be known as Fair Ground Road, as it led to the medieval fair, held from the early thirteenth century on land that is now occupied by the current General Post Office on Denby Dale Road and Gala Bingo. Beyond George Street and the River Chald was the Borough of Wakefield.

Old houses on Westgate, pictured c. 1900. Houses such as these were common in Wakefield during the medieval, Tudor and Stuart periods. It was only in the late Stuart and early Georgian period (c. 1680– 1720) that brick became used as the principal building material. From their appearance, these houses look to have been built in the 1560s, and survived until the twentieth century. Other timber-framed houses still exist on Northgate, Westgate and Silver Street, but many others have been demolished since 1940.

The expansion of nonconformity in the nineteenth century, and the building of new churches, meant that there was a need for clerical furnishings and fittings. Businesses were set up throughout Wakefield to cater for this need. The city became nationally famous for the building of one particular piece of church furniture: the pipe organ.

The population expansion of the nineteenth century required other services. Commerce expanded rapidly, and new shops needed suppliers for both their goods and their fittings. The 1920s saw a period where Victorian and pre-Victorian shop fronts and interiors were overhauled in the new Deco style. Again, Wakefield had one of the leading exponents of this new style of shop fitting – Drake & Warters Ltd. Slums were cleared and new housing estates were built on the fringe of the city at Lupset, Flanshaw, Portobello and elsewhere. To families moving to these new areas it must have seemed like paradise with large gardens and new modern houses, when compared with the old damp, cramped and decayed dwellings from where they had relocated.

The great depression of the 1920s affected every level of society, with many families leaving the area in search of work. After victory in the Second World War, reconstruction began. The old intimate streets, with their fine Victorian buildings were destroyed, making way, in the name of modernity, for shopping arcades.

The demolition of the Corn Exchange robbed the town of one of its finest buildings. The replanning and reconstruction of Wakefield over the last three decades has seen Wakefield becoming an increasingly important centre of nighttime entertainment with many nightclubs. The Ridings shopping centre, and the retail parks to the south of the city centre, provide jobs that were lost when the town's major industries of cloth, coal, corn and cattle collapsed.

Cross Square looking down Silver Street, c. 1900. The spire and tall-pitched roof in the background is the church institute, built on the site of the manor bakehouse. This scene is little different today, except that the building in the foreground is where Townsend the jewellers now stands. The corner of the current Barclays Bank building is visible on the extreme right of the image; next to it is the Black Swan Inn and the entrance to King Street.

Westgate Common with St Michael's Church in the distance, c. 1900. St Michael's was opened in 1866, near to the site of the chantry chapel of St Mary Magdalene, the site of which is to the left of the image. Visible along the right is Ings Beck. The houses on the left of the picture still stand, behind which, until recent times, stood the imposing bulk of M.P. Stonehouse's mill. This was one of many mills built on Westgate, Marriott's mill, Hayley's mill and Archer's mill being but three other examples.

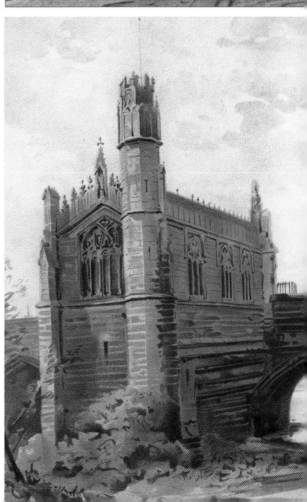

Above: *Warrengate and the Springs, c. 1900. Warrengate is either named after the Earls Warren or a rabbit warren. Warrengate was one of the principal streets of medieval Wakefield. The wall and trees to the right of the image are the Vicars' Croft burial ground and the Rectory Manor estate. The land is currently occupied by the Market Hall and car parks.*

Above right: *Butcher Row off Little Westgate, c. 1900. This, like Bread Street, was named after the produce that could be found here. At the end of the row can be seen the current Barclays Bank building.*

Right: *The Chantry Chapel of St Mary the Virgin, c. 1900. This was one of four similar chapels, but is the only one still standing. It was here, on New Year's Day 1460, that the young Earl of Rutland was dragged from sanctuary by Lord Clifford and the Lancastrian army, who had defeated the army of the Duke of York at Sandal. King Edward IV is believed to have ordered that prayers be offered for his father's and brother's souls. The Chantry was closed at the time of the Reformation, but was reopened in the mid-1840s after being restored by George Gilbert Scott. Above bridge level little of the medieval building survives. The current façade is twentieth century.*

Boots the Chemist, Westgate, a typical Art Deco building, 1938.

The Six Chimneys, Kirkgate, 1943. This was one of the finest timber-framed buildings in Wakefield until it collapsed in that year after years of neglect and structural alteration, which left it unstable.

Right: *Passage leading to Westgate from Westmoreland Street.*

Below: *The Shepherd's Rest, Fair Ground Road, c. 1890.*

Looking down King Street towards the Town Hall, c. 1920.

1

Local Community & Daily Life

L ife in the past is not always as romantic as it seems in photographs and old films. Existence was hard, with few, if any, labour saving devices being affordable before the 1960s. The day-to-day life of many working-class communities living in Wakefield in the 1950s had changed very little in more than three generations. Everything was done by hand: washing, cleaning and cooking. Transport was either by foot or public transport; few people were lucky enough to own their own car. Some families still kept a pony and trap. The building of the new council estates cleared the city centre slums, and a new community was built at Lupset.

> Not long ago the parish of Lupset consisted entirely of rough pasture. Today it is a thriving residential area with 1,500 houses, with gardens back and front, making it a veritable garden city, and one of the finest municipal housing estates in the north of England. Almost every house is fitted with a bath and there is such a plethora of buses.
>
> *Wakefield Express*

Many of the electrical goods now taken for granted did not exist fifty years ago, although some had been available before the outbreak of the Second World War. Electric food mixers had been available before the conflicts, as were vacuum cleaners and electric lawnmowers. Of course these were only available for the wealthy. These white goods were unobtainable to most households until the 1960s and 1970s. Mrs Shirley Murdock recalls that her father gave her mother an electric mixer for her birthday in 1939. It was of little use, except that it was used to make butter during the war from the cream that had been collected off the daily milk. The cream was then stored up and used when enough had been amassed.

> . . . by 1934, trams no longer ran down Horbury Road and were replaced by red double decker buses, which served the nearly completed Lupset housing estate. Trams disappeared soon after the Second World War.
>
> *Ruth Tetley*

In the last century the workers' houses were generally two bedrooms and built of stone to the west of Wakefield and brick to the north and east. They lacked all modern amenities. No water taps and no lavatories, but a dry ash closet at the bottom of the street shared by neighbours. The houses in the main were kept scrupulously clean indoors – and outdoors the flags and windowsills were always well scoured. Water was carried from wells in the villages or communal pumps in Wakefield itself, and was the cause of much illness. The death rate amongst children was very high. Dirty water was disposed of down roadside gutters, which soaked back into the ground to be consumed again without any cleaning, lighting was by a green flame from a few gas lights, or, for the very poor, by candles. Monday was always washday with the washing being strung across the road between the terraces of houses. After the First World War, new council houses were built which had running water. Some had a bath in the scullery though the lavatory was often in an outhouse or a shed at the bottom of the garden.

Eric Swinden

Heating was by coal fire which had to be set every day in the winter. We were lucky and this was done by the maid, at about six o'clock in the morning, so the room was warm when you got up about an hour later. In the summer a folded paper fan was often placed in the grate. Of course all the grates in the house had to be 'Zeboed' with black lead once a week to keep them clean. Zeboe was like black shoe polish for cast-iron fireplaces. It was put on with a cloth and then buffed off with a stiff bristled brush. We also did not have the luxury of stainless steel pans. They were either copper or enamelled, copper ones having to be cleaned once a week with Brasso. Cleaning was a major part of any day, there being no labour saving devices. All carpets had to be swept by hand; everything had to be cleaned daily due to the soot from the coal fires. Cleaning the flues was very important; if not, the build-up of soot would prevent the fire from burning properly, and if so much built up it could drop, filling the house with black soot. Once a year after Christmas, the house would be thoroughly cleaned from top to bottom, and, where necessary, new wallpaper and paint applied. Carpets and rugs would be taken up and hung on the washing line and beaten with a carpet beater to remove dirt. This was known as spring-cleaning and was a major undertaking.

Shirley Murdock

Middle and upper class housing was built throughout Wakefield in the Georgian era, c. 1926. The developments at St Johns and here at South Parade epitomise this style of architecture.

After the passing of the Housing and Town Planning Act in 1919, Wakefield Council set about the construction of full-scale housing estates, having previously experimented with houses on Elm Tree Street in Belle Vue and Rufford Street in Alverthorpe. The first estate was built at Portobello and, in 1920, the council approached the owners of Portobello House for the purchase of the estate with the house and garden remaining intact. Tenders for the new council houses had to be submitted to the Ministry of Health before the local authority could accept them. When the bidding began on the contract, the Wakefield Master Builders Federation expected to be given the contract as they had built the earlier houses in Belle Vue and Alverthorpe. These new houses at Portobello were some of the first houses in Wakefield to be purpose-built with electric lighting and gas for cooking. There was also provision for a coal fire in the living room and a master bedroom. The estate also was to contain shops, a pub and a school. It was the yardstick by which all subsequent council estates would be judged. These new houses were a dramatic improvement on the damp and squalid conditions of the inner city housing stock. However, though condemned and demolished, the redevelopment of the city centre did not take place until the 1950s.

It was a familiar sight to see horse-drawn wagonettes carrying people to Wakefield or Leeds on shopping days and to see footballers and cricketers travelling to away matches by this means. Excursions were also organised using this means of transport to places no further away than Roundhay Park or Soothill Gardens. For private trips both a dogcart and a landau were available. Trams came to Wakefield by 1905, but not to many of the surrounding villages. By the 1920s, solid-tyre buses had been replaced by pneumatic-tyre buses, by the West Riding Omnibus Company, to the surrounding villages, and, by 1924, they had over 200 buses in operation in Wakefield and environs. Fred was a drayman/shunter for the railway. As a four-year-old I remember being on the dray once when he was delivering through the Stork Gates to Thornes House, when, going up the slope, the horse was skidding and sparks were flying from the hooves. At the back of Kirkgate station I had to go to the stables at the top of the station yard, and I was clinging on for dear life because I was miles high. There was a room attached to the stables (presumably a tack room), with horse collars hung around and a bright yellow, hissing, gas lamp.

Ron Swinden

Horse and trap, c. 1935. For many people this was the only way that they could afford their own transport.

A day out, c. 1935. This family was lucky enough, in the 1930s, to be able to afford a car to go on day trips to the coast.

A young girl posing by her father's Jaguar on Horbury Road, c. 1942.

A Wolseley car outside a house on Horbury Road, c. 1938.

A lot of goods were also bought and sold on the doorstep. Mrs Shirley Murdock recalls that 'Whitakers Dairy was supplied by milk from Haigh Park Farm near Walton. The milkman would come down Horbury Road, from Horbury, with his horse and cart, the milk being transported in metal milk churns that clanged and banged with every movement of the cart. The milkman would then come to the door, or the housewife into the street with a large jug. The milk was then ladled from a large can; the jug being filled with fresh milk, there was no green-top or red-top in those days. This took place every day except Sundays, there being no supermarkets. This continued into the early 1950s.'

In 1932, Wakefield Borough Cooperative Society opened a new dairy at Lupset, with a pasteurising plant, and soon became the largest milk retailers for Wakefield. Gone were the milk churns, as new glass pint milk bottles were introduced with paper tops, which became a common sight on many doorsteps. Almost as familiar as the milkmen were the greengrocers and other tradesmen:

Mr Minnett was a market gardener who sold his wares from the back of a horse-drawn cart. Other goods were sold in the street, again from carts. Mr Grange had an egg round and there was also a yeast round. The yeast man was a veteran of the Great War and was disabled, selling his yeast from his wheelchair; he would ring his bell, to inform the housewife of his presence outside their door. This was in the days when nearly every house made its own bread every day. Two ounces cost about 4d. A knife sharpener would also visit at least once a week, as would a pot man, who sold cooking pots and pans. Midweek, a grocer and butcher from Horbury also came round. For other items mother always used to telephone Webster's in Wakefield, to place her order, and it would be delivered the same day, either by a boy on a bicycle or a small van. Webster's had three shops. Webster's Brothers refreshment rooms and Bensons Confectioners were neighbours in Cross Square. Mrs Benson was bought out by Webster's in the 1930s and opened the ground floor shop as a large grocers, and the upstairs as a tearoom. Webster's also had a branch at 202 Kirkgate as well as 70 Westgate. Other shops at the time were Simpson's shoe shop on the corner of Westmoreland Street and Brook Street, Burtons and Pickles & Sons tailors. Mr Pickles was from West Parade chapel and had been a Mayor of Wakefield.

Most weeks followed the same pattern: Tuesday was washday, Wednesday ironing day, Thursday flue day and Friday backing day as the oven burnt the hottest due to the flues being cleaned. The bread dough was made on the Thursday and was a good way of cleaning your hands from the soot from the flues. Ninety per cent of the week's bread, cakes and pies would be made on the Friday and stored in the pantry during the week to keep it fresh. Fresh bread could be purchased from bakeries in Wakefield if you ran out or could afford to do so. All cooking was done on a coal- or oil-fired range, either by Aga, Rayburn or, in older homes, a traditional cast-iron Yorkshire range. All meals were made from scratch. You decided what you were going to eat for the evening meal, purchased the ingredients in the morning and, after dinner, made the evening meal. Frozen ready meals were not invented, so cookbooks like Mrs Beeton's were the bible of the kitchen.

Shirley Murdock

Window shopping, c. 1950. This well-dressed man is shopping for a new suit at Burtons.

In the surrounding villages like Horbury and Outwood, everyday commodities could be purchased locally. Wakefield was accessible by bus, or train for Alverthorpe, Stanley and Lofthouse/Outwood for buying of larger items such as furniture, the buying of which was usually prefaced by shop window gazing and price comparisons. For many folk, a shopping spree in Wakefield, like today, was an antidote to the dull routine of everyday life. Who could resist Redman's in Upper Kirkgate for fresh sliced bacon or loose dried fruit from an excellent counter display? The market held on Saturdays was second to none and lasted into the evening.

Ruth Tetley

The Grand Clothing Hall on the corner of Mary Gate and Westgate, c. *1930.*

Schofield's, c. 1950. This was a very upmarket shop selling ready-made clothes, material and bespoke clothing, primarily ladies' dresses.

Noel Fashions. This was situated on the corner of Northgate and Mary Gate. They specialised in ready made, off-the-peg clothing. By the 1950s, few people had their clothes made individually for them by a tailor.

Timothy Whites & Taylors, c. 1950. This was one of many independent chemists in Wakefield at the time.

Right: *Interior of Timothy Whites & Taylors. They dealt not only with prescriptions and medicines, but also sold sweets and other remedies.*

Judge's Dispensing Chemists, c. 1950.

2

Leisure in Bygone Days

Before the invention of motor transport, radio and television, how did Wakefield folk manage to pass their time? For many communities the church or chapel was the centre of activities. The many Methodists in the city and the surrounding villages took the temperance oath and abstained from alcohol. Aside from them, particularly for men, the pub was an important part of life. Beyond the pub, the cinema was always an attraction for some hours of diversion.

Mr Ron Swinden was born in 1923 in Wakefield. He was a member of the league of abstainers, like many of the Methodists of his generation, and was teetotal until the day he died.

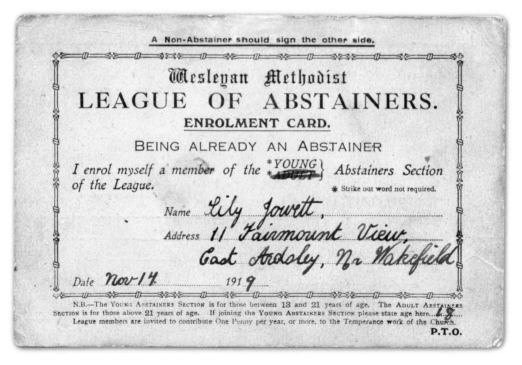

This is a membership card for the Wesleyan Methodist League of Abstainers dated 17 November 1919. Upon enrolment the member had to pledge 'I promise to abstain by the help of God from all intoxicating liquors and beverages'.

That the poverty, hardship and illness they endured never overwhelmed them is certain. When people talk of the good old days, do they remember the slum areas in Northgate, Kirkgate, Eastmoor, and Westgate with houses infested with lice and often rats? Do they remember the sanitary conditions, the needs of the sick and poor? Until their pocket money was exhausted many men spent their leisure time in one of Wakefield's pubs. Wages were low; a farm labourer could earn 15s a week; 30s was considered a good wage before the First World War. Even good lawyers could only expect to take home about £3 a week. I was born in 1923 and I well remember the hardships resulted by the Great Depression in the late 1920s and early 1930s. Many Wakefield families left the area, especially miners, to seek work elsewhere. Hams could be bought for 10s, coal for 10s a ton, and best suits from the tailors for £2 10s. Whiskey cost 2s 6d a bottle, beer 1d a glass, thick twist tobacco 1s 2d.

Before the First World War, public houses were open to 11 p.m., and men went out sober at 8 or 9 p.m. and were conveyed home drunk at closing time. In both town and village, weekends were especially lively, rowdy times with singing, shouting and heated arguments, broadcast in broad Yorkshire dialect, often ending up with quarrels, which were settled outdoors with a rough and tumble fight, with no more serious injury than one or two bleeding noses.

Ron Swinden

The cinema revolutionised social life in Wakefield and the surrounding areas in the twentieth century. The first picture house in Wakefield was the Hippodrome on Teal Street. The building initially opened to provide equestrian and acrobatic entertainment but began to show films from 1906 under the direction of Sydney Tolfree. A year later, Excelsior Pictures hired the Unity Hall for a week, with the Corn Exchange being hired by the St Louis Animated Picture Company.

The first real competition to the Hippodrome was Benjamin Sherwood's Empire Cinema, which opened in Kirkgate in December 1909. It was a very different affair to Tolfree's wood and iron Hippodrome. The Electric Theatre was soon set up in the saloon of the Corn Exchange, and was Wakefield's first exclusively cinematic venture. In 1912, the Tivoli, later the Carlton, was opened on Grove Road, off Kirkgate. A year later, Tolfree purchased the site for his new cinema – the Picture House – at the top of Westgate. Today, the building merits a place in the Upper Westgate conservation area. It cost £13,000 to build and could seat 1,460 people. Like the Empire it had an orchestra from the outset.

The end of the First World War saw a new boom time in cinema. In the early 1920s, the Coliseum was built in Stanley Road next to Eastmoor Wesleyan Methodist Church. The Stanley Picture House, the Palace Cinema Belle Vue, the

The Picture House, Westgate, c. *1930.*

The Savoy cinema, Horbury Road, during demolition, c. *1995.*

Savoy Lupset and the Outwood Empire also all opened in the twenties. The Picture House, known as the Playhouse, was renovated in 1921, when a Conacher organ was introduced. Eric Bradley noted that the instrument was eminently suitable for performances of cantatas or oratorios, and was an organ in a cinema, rather than a cinema organ per se. In 1929, the Picture House was again at the forefront of cinematic experiences in Wakefield when it was wired for sound.

For many years, one of the most familiar and pleasant sounds in summer was the sound of bat against ball on the cricket pitches of the many villages surrounding Wakefield. Any time of the day in summer, except Sundays, men would be found practising in the nets. It was a period when getting into the Third XI was an achievement. In 1895, Stanley won the Wakefield and District Cup under the captaincy of the church curate. The curate, Mr Kingston, not only led the team, but also controlled the large and enthusiastic crowd of spectators, on occasions threatening expulsion from the field if the language was not moderated. At Wrenthorpe, Outwood and Kirkhamgate the Methodists were the cricketing entrepreneurs. At Kirkhamgate, one of the saddest losses during the war was Squadron Leader Maurice Pickersgill. He was acknowledged by everyone to have been a great sportsman, with a tremendous ability at cricket and football. Ron Swinden attended the same school – Thornes House Boys Secondary School – and was able to observe his prowess. He was also choirmaster at Kirkhamgate Reheboth Methodist Church. Ron Swinden's game was tennis and he reached the final of the Wakefield tennis competition for youth clubs in 1941, but, on the day of the final, was called up into the RAF, so could not compete.

> Football was another popular sport and players could be seen training during the week in winter in the football field, which at Stanley adjoined the cricket field. The village could muster two teams and these were well supported by spectators in the Sunday match. Rugby was as popular as now, if not more so, with the local team, Wakefield Trinity Dreadnoughts, winning the cup in 1947.
>
> 'Knur and spell' was played any time of the week, both summer and winter – using both cricket and football fields. This was played with an adjustable spell on a wooden base spiked into the ground, with a steel spring fixed on the top. When a trigger on the spell was tapped, it released the taut spring, and, from a cap on the end of the spring, a knur, or potty, was tossed into the air and with a long handled pummel the player made a mighty swipe at the knur to try and knock it as far as possible.
>
> *Ron Swinden*

Mr Swinden notes that Stanley had some notable players and contests were often arranged with players from neighbouring villages. A familiar shout on these occasions was 'reit ower year' (right over here).

Miss Pickles playing cricket in Wakefield Park, c. 1920. Her father, Samuel Pickles, was a gentlemen's outfitter and mayor of Wakefield, as well as being a trustee of West Parade Methodist Church.

There was an unwritten code that when the seasons changed so did the games that we used to play. Strange isn't it, as for months one game would be predominant and then overnight, without any communication, we all brought the same to school. Skipping was popular, as was marbles, jacks, hopscotch and others.

Shirley Murdock

Another of the popular pastimes which was practised in any corner of the town or nearby villages at any time, any day, summer or winter, when two or more men gathered together, was 'pitch and toss'. When played in the village street, look-out men would be stationed at strategic points to warn of the approach of the village policeman, as, many times, prosecution and fines followed when men were caught playing this game.

Children's pastimes were, as always and everywhere, more varied. Not being allowed to play in the cricket field, they did not wait for the provision of playing fields or expensive equipment, but made use of home-made equipment, including a crewelled ball and played cricket on any suitable piece of vacant land such as Papes Hill, the 'Plantin', the quarry. Any summer's evening half a dozen games would be going on in different places. Traffic was practically non-existent and cricket was played on the highway (if the policeman was not about). Other popular games played with do-it-yourself equipment were 'duckstone' and 'kick-aht-can'.

Ron Swinden

Tennis, c. 1935. Some middle-class homes had private tennis courts. Here we see two groups of children using the court in the garden of 6 South Parade.

Riding was also a popular pastime. Here we see two sisters at Lupset Farm, c. 1943.

A young girl tacking her horse at Lupset Farm.

Lupset Farm, c. 1943. Today these green fields have been built on with modern housing.

Feeding the ducks in Thornes Park, c. 1950. As it is today, the park was popular with Wakefield residents of all ages.

The Heath Common fair was also popular. Here we see a steam-powered carousel, c. 1935.

The fair also had numerous sideshows; this one is a postcard stand.

GROW YOUR OWN

Much leisure time was spent, by many of the miners of Stanley, in an old quarry. Some would meet in the 'Tabernacle' (a wooden hut). Many of them, being unable to read, would welcome anyone who was literate to entertain them from books and newspapers. In parts of this quarry, where suitable soil could be found, allotment gardens were cultivated. Easter Holiday Monday, whether early or late, was the day for potato planting, and a large number of men would be there: gardeners, helpers and onlookers who no doubt acted as advisers.

Another way of providing food for many of the large, often poor, families was to rear pigs. So popular was pig keeping that it was customary, when building a house, to fix plenty of bricks into the beams that supported the ceiling on which to hang hams and rolls of bacon, and to build a pigsty at the bottom of the garden. The pigs were killed in the owner's backyard. Many people kept poultry to supplement the food supply, and some men . . . could build a poultry shed with any odds and ends of timber or empty boxes and a saw, hammer and nails. Many people also tended allotments to grow vegetables; of course during the war many pristine lawns and flowerbeds were replaced by allotment gardens.

Rabbit coursing and pigeon shoots were sometimes organised in the cricket field. Businessmen would often go on hunting parties at many of the large country houses near Wakefield such as Nostell Priory, the seat of Lord and Lady St Oswald. One of the pleasant sights of summer was to see circling round the village flocks of pigeons, or to see men near a pigeon cote waiting and watching expectantly for the arrival home of pigeons which had been sent away for a pigeon race. But sunshine or not the pigeon fanciers could be seen walking with a small basket, or riding a bicycle on which was strapped a larger basket, or pushing a pair of wheels on which was a larger basket still. Those baskets contained pigeons which were taken for a distance, then released for the purpose of training them to fly back to the pigeon cote as quickly as possible, or sending them away – in some cases overseas – for a pigeon race. On the arrival of the pigeons after a race men would be seen scurrying along with timing clocks in their hands to a place of rendezvous. How long pigeon fanciers have been in Lee Moor no one knows, but pigeons have won many prizes for their enthusiastic owners. The middle classes were often involved with the local fox hunt, and would spend weekends away carrying out business at shooting parties held in the local big houses.

Ron Swinden

A shooting party of Wakefield businessmen, c. *1950.*

Repairing a garden terrace wall, c. *1950. In the postwar years gardening became a very popular pastime.*

A father and his two daughters relaxing in the garden after a hard morning's work on the vegetable patch, c. 1935.

A family gathering, c. 1935. The garden became a place for the family to meet and enjoy themselves – a sort of outside room.

Charlie Drake, local entrepreneur, posing proudly by the fruits of his hard labour in the garden, c. *1935.*

A spaniel, apparently needing glasses and with the ability to take photographs, has these young sisters mesmerised.

The garden was also a place of recreation. Here a young girl has the luxury of both a swing and a seesaw in her garden.

A boy standing proudly by his parents' vegetable patch, c. 1930.

Snow made gardens a winter wonderland. Here we see two young girls posing by their artistic creation in the snow.

The winter of 1943 was severe, as demonstrated by the depth of snow seen here.

Wine Lodge Yard and a snowbound Wakefield, 1943.

Looking up Almshouse Lane towards Westgate, 1943.

A TRIP TO THE PICTURES

Mrs Ruth Tetley was born in Wakefield and lived on Horbury Road, between Horbury and Wakefield. She recalls that her local cinema was the Savoy Cinema (seen on p. 32), which was unusual as it had a sloping floor and no gallery:

Saturdays were often spent in the cinema, and six films were often shown in succession. You got real value for money: tickets cost 2d. Buck Jones and Roy Rogers were the favourites at the time. The showing often consisted of three features, a newsreel – there being no television news then – a review, a cartoon and of course ice cream. The treat of the week was our Saturday night visit to the local cinema where we had reserved seats.

We could also go roller skating at the Roller Drome in the Corn Exchange. The Corn Exchange also had the Grand Electric cinema, owned by the same people as the Picture House. It was in the upper saloon, a huge space with ornately moulded ceiling plaster, and vast windows. It was pulled down in the 1970s to make way for C&As. It was a spectacular building.

Ruth Tetley

The Gaumont cinema, Kirkgate, c. 1940.

The Star cinema, Eastmoor, c. 1940.

The Regal cinema, Kirkgate. The picture-house was showing Burt Lancaster in His Majesty O'Keefe *at the time the photograph was taken in 1954.*

Mr David Murdock adds that: 'the main feature film was usually preceded by a cartoon and a newsreel but the news was usually old by the time we saw it. If we missed a film, we could always see it at another cinema during the week.'

The decline of the cinema with the advent of television in the 1950s led to the sale and closure of all of Wakefield's cinemas except the Regal. Even the more richly appointed Theatre Royal and Opera House was closed and became a bingo hall. Mrs Jane Dawson notes that when the picture house closed as a cinema in 1977, it became a skateboard centre, and then a nightclub that was famous throughout Yorkshire. It was called 'Rooftop Gardens, and was on a par with Batley Variety Club in attracting the celebrities of the day; it was the place to be seen. Downstairs was another nightclub, Casanova's. On Ings Road, the pig market was replaced with a bowling alley. Bowling was one of the crazes of the late 1950s and 1960s; it was the first in the area. It eventually became a bingo hall in the early 1980s.'

In the middle years of the twentieth century, virtually every home had a wireless.

Before the television became a mass medium, the wireless was a source of both news and entertainment. For children the adventures of Romany and his dog were very popular. Romany, a.k.a. the Revd Bramwell Evans, was a Methodist minister, and laid the foundations of Wesley Hall church in the 1930s and preached at West Parade. That must have been after the war. So popular was the radio that Wesley Hall had a radio installed in the Sunday School and teachers' common room. Swimming was also popular. There was not mixed bathing on those days. Wakefield, as today, had two swimming pools, the current one on Sun Lane, and the old Victorian one on Almshouse Lane, where we would go from school when I was in lower IV. Sisset baths allowed mix bathing, and we went before school. Of course we could also go to the seaside, more often than not Filey on the east coast where my parents had a bungalow, by car or train.

Shirley Murdock

Dancing was also very popular before and after the war. 'Hops' were held in St George's Hall, Lupset, a good dance band always being in attendance. Hops were also held in the Mechanics Institute, which is now Wakefield Museum, the Assembly Rooms, which was the former Town Hall on King Street, and the Unity Hall. Subscription dances were very popular after the war.

Ruth Tetley

The interior of the Unity Hall set up for a dinner dance, c. 1950.

During the war, fundraising dances were held for Warship Week, Spitfire Week, and, for the elite of society, the Mayor's Ball. Dances were also held at the Unity Hall to raise funds for the war effort, and were organised by Charlie Drake and others. A band was always present and Mr Mathewman was the MC.

After the war, the Unity Hall was also used as a venue for plays, and was used as the venue for the Wakefield Schools Festival Choir, which was nothing very special really and a poor imitation of similar events in Pontefract and Manchester. The Dream of Gerontius was once presented at the Unity Hall, though it was overshadowed by the Yorkshire Symphony Orchestra's performance of Handel's *Messiah* at the Picture House. Isobel Bailey and Kathleen Ferrier were the leads, and I think my cousin, Eric Bradley, was the organist.

The Picture House was always a far more classy venue than either the Unity Hall or Theatre Royal, and hosted many choral works and high opera productions, it having more seating and better acoustics than the Theatre Royal. The organ was an extra bonus. It really was a better venue.

For amateur dramatics, the Queen Street Hall was an excellent venue after the war of course. This was converted from the Market Street Primitive Methodist church, and Drake & Warters provided the backdrops for the first production in 1955. They were painted by Frank Bateson, who was a real artist.

The Regal was also used as a venue for theatre as I remember going to see *1066 and All That* and other productions there. Singing and drama took up a lot of people's time, what with singing in the chapel or church choir, the Wakefield Choral Society, Wakefield Sylvian Operatic Society or the Gilbert & Sullivan society. Wakefield was once a very musical town.

Shirley Murdock

Walking was popular as now, and was the main form of getting around for many people. I remember that we walked all over the place with the youth club from St George's Church. Once we walked to Cannon Hill Park, near Barnsley, and we took our own picnic with us. We spent the afternoon in the park, and then got a charabanc back to Wakefield to attend the 'hop' in the church hall at the night.

We would also often get the tram into Wakefield and walk back to Horbury after we had been shopping or visiting friends.

During the war these day trips to nearby places became popular due to a campaign called 'Holidays at Home'. A special week of activities was held in 1943 and was held in Thornes Park.

Also held in the park on most Sunday afternoons was a brass band concert in the bandstand at the bottom of Cannon Ball Hill. You always had to be well dressed, and we often took a picnic with us. The bands often came from the local pits.

An annual event on the calendar was the Miners' Gala. It was a very large affair with banners and many brass bands. The procession would leave Wood Street, go down Market Street and then march to the arena in Clarence Park. Here a gala was held with different stalls and games, all to raise money for miners' welfare. Mining was once a major industry for Wakefield and area. A brass band from one of the many pits in the area would often give a concert in the bandstand.

Ruth Tetley

3

Religious Life: Church & Chapel

The preface to the 1933 Methodist Hymn Book states: 'Methodism was born in song', and all of Wakefield's Methodist churches tried to prove this. With the conversion of John and Charles Wesley in 1738, a new form of evangelical Christianity was born – Methodism. The Wesleys' interpretation of the scriptures challenged all those who heard them to reform their lives through repentance based on a Christian method, advocated by them and laid out in the Bible. The Wesleys' theology was Anglican in basis, but it was presented in a fashion that brought hope to the poorer and middle classes. The simple call of fair play, clean living and living life by the Christian method appealed to all regardless of rank.

West Parade Chapel, c. 1803. West Parade was opened in 1802, and was built to a design by Mr Watson of Doncaster that had been prepared for nearby St John's Church. To mark the centenary of Wesleyan Methodism in 1839, the building was enlarged to seat a congregation of nearly 2,000.

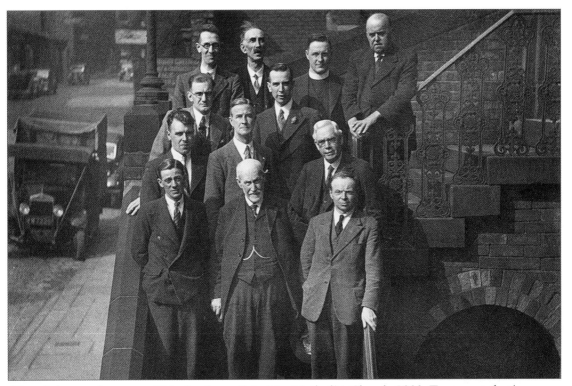

The minister and trustees of Market Street Primitive Methodist Church, 1933. Trustees at the time were Fred Laughton, Harry Dawson, William A. Brownlow, Joseph A. Carr, Herbert Garwell, Cecil Brownlow, Harold Mitchell, Donald C. Dawson, Robert Macmillan, Harold Mosley, Sydney H. Butler, Alfred B. Durry and John W. Barker. Samuel Seal was also a member and trustee here. The first Primitive Methodist Church was opened on 30 November 1823 on Quebec Street. This chapel was too large for the congregation, with seating for 600 worshippers. In 1836, it was decided to build the present Market Street building, which was opened on 16 December 1838. The Baptists used the Quebec Street chapel until their new building on George Street was completed in 1844. The chapel interior was moved, in 1865, to Mr Oakes's private chapel at Flanshaw. The building today is Flanshaw Congregational Church, and many of the 1823 fittings remain. The Market Street chapel was enlarged and renovated when the present Market Street façade was built. Robert Bownas Mackie, a noted Wesleyan Methodist, laid the foundation stones. The newly enlarged chapel could seat a congregation of 350, which merged with West Parade in 1954, and the building became the Queen Street Hall.

In later decades, this responsibility fell to the Band of Hope and the Wesleyan Methodist League of Abstainers.

Wherever they preached, followers flocked to hear, and, once satiated, continued their work. From Cornwall to Northumbria they lustily worked their way towards progress, and, in a space of a very few years, societies and chapels were established in towns, cities and the humblest villages. Wakefield was no exception.

In a very short space of time, meeting houses and chapels replaced barns and stables, all vibrating with congregations eager to sing of the joys of the Christian life, despite the drudgery of their daily existence.

Methodism came early to Wakefield. The first chapel was opened in 1774 on Thornhill Street. West Parade Chapel, the mother for numerous smaller chapels, replaced this.

The town centre had no fewer than five Methodist chapels: West Parade Wesleyans built in 1802, Market Street Primitives built in 1838 and renovated in 1880, Market Street United Methodists built in 1857, the Methodist New Connexion Church was opened in Grove Road on 15 February 1866 and a United Methodist Church was built on Saville Street in 1876, which became known as Brunswick. Wesleyan chapels were also built at Westgate End and Eastmoor. As well as the Methodists, Wakefield had three Congregational Churches: Zion and Salem on George Street, and John Street Chapel. The Baptist chapel was also on George

METHODIST CHAPELS

West Parade was a huge chapel, soundly built, with red mahogany seating and two wide staircases to the upper floor with a further staircase to the choir stalls at the rear probably capable of seating 100 choristers. The centrepiece was a huge pulpit for almost twenty preachers and a magnificent organ usually played by N.K. Shrigley FRCO. Earlier in the century, Albert Sugden had been the organist. The congregational area was probably some 1,000 seats, mostly family pews. Across the side road was an equally imposing Sunday school with many classrooms and larger rooms capable of being used for meetings plus extensive cellars. All large areas to keep clean but invaluable for circuit functions.

I well remember a full week of a missionary exhibition suggested by a scholar, Kenneth Holt, and teacher and JMA leader, Marion Jacques, both of Westgate End, which provided artefacts and speakers from all the colonies of the British Empire. Every room within the Sunday school was put to use for demonstration purposes re India, Africa, China, British Honduras and so on. All the valuable exhibits were transported from the Methodist Missionary Society in London. Missionaries such as Mary Slessor of Calabar, Grenfell of Labrador were, in their absence, congratulated on their successful spreading of the gospel to heathen lands. Mr Seiles was one of the coordinators assisted by J.W. Dale.

Ron Swinden

Opposite: *Interior of West Parade, 1901. This photograph shows the interior after the renovations of 1896, when the mahogany pews, gallery face and fittings were installed. The organ case dates from 1824 and housed three successive organs: the first by Joseph Booth, the second by Francis Booth of 1839 and the last by an organ of 1880, built by Isaac Abbott of Leeds. Organists here included J.N.O. Hardy, who departed in 1888 to become the first cathedral organist, and Albert Edward Sutcliffe Sugden, his successor until 1921.*

West Parade's eighteen class leaders included physicians, bankers, the governor of the House of Correction, manufacturers, shopkeepers, and that the chapel's members were foremost in charitable works outside the church, though its fashionable ostentatiousness, coupled with high seat rents, excluded the working classes. West Parade was the 'largest and most handsome' chapel in Wakefield and its members included Thomas and John Tootal.

John Cryer, 1835

Street. The city centre also boasted six churches and chapels in addition to the cathedral: St John the Baptist, St Mark's, St Mary (Primrose Hill), St Mary the Virgin (Chantry Chapel), St Andrew's and Holy Trinity. The Catholic church was on Wentworth Terrace, the Unitarian on Westgate, the Spiritualist on Queen Street, the Salvation Army on Eastmoor and the mental institution had a non-denominational chapel dedicated to St Faith.

Westgate End was founded in 1813, but it was not until 1827 that the Revd Joseph Agar decided to build the present chapel there. The building was renovated internally in 1886, and closed in 1993. Ron Swinden noted that Westgate End was similar to West Parade with a relatively new Sunday school (built in 1909). Here again congregations were not small, with family connections clearly continuing by generations. 'I well remember the older men of my youth. Such stalwarts as Messrs Ross, Fletcher, Glover, Archer, Hoyles, Hames, Harvey, Dixon, Stead, Ayers, Perkins, Darling, and Clark, and Mesdames Houle, Hames, Archer, Dixon, Stead, plus my aunts Clarke and Lodge, all part of a vibrant chapel congregation supported by a Wesley Guild, a magnificent choir and a young men's class containing Joe Mann, Dick Dutton, Gordon Atkinson, Eric Bradley, Clifford Lee, the three Clark brothers, Harry Just, George Hyde and my brothers Stanley and Leslie. Services were always well attended with good choirmasters and organists ever ready to organise the singing using the Abbott and Smith organ, inflated by the caretaker's sons, or later by myself and twin brother Eric. Some organists I remember were Gerald Raper, Arnold Roberts ARCO, Eric Bradley, Clifford Lee, George Glover, H.M. Woodhead, Arnold Swallow and John Newsome.'

At Westgate End the great musical theme of Methodism was upheld. The choirs, choirmasters and organists always gave a good lead to hymn singing and also regularly provided anthems, which were stored away in a large cupboard, among a large and well-preserved variety. On special occasions, Handel's *Messiah*, Haydn's *Creation* and Mendelssohn's *Elijah* were regular oratorios produced in the early years, but smaller productions like John Stainer's *Crucifixion*, *Olivet to Calvary* and the *Children's Messiah* came some time later. One could also depend upon a wide variety of local preachers and ministers who served the congregation with distinction.

Extra collections were taken at communion services to provide a 'poor fund', which was used to subsidise the needy families in the chapel community and the

West Parade, c. 1920. This photograph shows both the chapel and the Sunday school. West Parade was closed in 1966 and the congregation merged with nearby Grove Road Chapel. Both chapel and school have now been demolished, robbing Wakefield of its finest Georgian churches.

surrounding area. During the General Strike of 1926, and the Depression years that followed, the local authority, distributing dole money to miners experiencing hard times, used the Sunday school premises. It was not unusual to see pit names such as Manor, Walton or Parkhill on the collection plate each Sunday for many months.

Concerts and an occasional bazaar were also regularly held to supplement chapel funds and special needs. These necessitated the frames and trestle tables that were stored in the spacious cellars. Heating both chapel and school was a continuing chore but was efficiently carried out by the caretakers, Mr and Mrs Hutchinson, who lived in a chapel-owned property, 12 Morton Parade, Westgate.

In early Sunday school days, Lawrence Swinden was the superintendent, with Ted Shutt and Arnold Roberts sometimes officiating. They were assisted at the grand piano by Edith M. Cameron, with Mildred and Muriel Latham and Irene Law (née Carver), as junior choir leaders. The attendance at Sunday school in the early years was well over 100 scholars. After attending the morning service, they returned in the afternoon to hear some brilliant singing from the Methodist Sunday school hymnal, led by the superintendent. Numbers 380 and 407 were popular requests. The primary department was conducted in separate rooms and was led by Alice Dunnil and Marion Jacques using hymns on printed rolls; the favourite hymn was 'When Mothers of Salem'. Sunday school lessons were often somewhat farcical as some teachers, after a short attempt to get scholars to read the tatty bibles, relied on Enid

Interior of West Parade, c. 1930. Harvest festivals have always been special services. Here we see the table and pulpit platform profusely decorated with produce. The pulpit platform was built in the 1920s out of the old, three-level pulpit of 1839.

Blyton stories or indulged in current topics that provided commentaries on daily life. At a convenient time, the Sunday school superintendent would push a variety of bell buttons indicating to each class that they should return to the main hall for further singing, vespers or notices. At the age of fourteen, each scholar was expected to take charge of a class of young children.

At the rear of the main Sunday school hall two large pictures contained photos of members of the chapel and Sunday school who had served in the First World War (1914–18). One displayed those who had perished and the other those who had survived, which included the former superintendent, Gilbert Howarth. At Gallipoli Herbert Clark lost an arm and Clement Bradley his left leg, which was replaced by a cork substitute that he used with commendable ease.

At one time Alverthorpe had two chapels: one was on Batley Road and the other at New Scarborough, built midway into Regent Street. Here Miss Swale, the daughter of T. Swale, a confectioner from Alverthorpe Road, led the congregation. She remembers asking his mother to play the piano for her mid-week ladies' meetings.

The minister and his wife outside Regent Street Chapel, New Scarborough, c. 1910. This little chapel was opened on 17 July 1874. There had been a Primitive Methodist society in Alverthorpe since 1811. The chapel was closed in 1939. It was reopened in the early 1950s by Leslie Jacques as the Bethel Memorial Mission.

That would have been in about 1929. Subsequently Ron Swinden remembers attending a meeting organised by Cliff College Treckers at which Blinco, Jack Ward, Herbert Silverwood and others exhorted the local population to give their support. Later, a Mr Casburn tried to keep this small chapel going. But ultimately, Westgate End and Alverthorpe survived while New Scarborough chapel was closed and became used by George Gilbey & Sons to store furniture. It was later demolished. The Gilbey family were staunch supporters of Zion Congregational Church in George Street.

Mr Swinden joined the Royal Air Force in 1943 and returned to Westgate End in 1947. Upon his return he was immediately appointed as a junior teacher in the Sunday school along with Reg Browning during Fred Lunn's period as super-intendent. Many Wakefield children who had grown up and joined the armed services returned from the battlegrounds in 1945, so the Sunday school grew by leaps and bounds, and soon numbered over 100 scholars again. In 1948, the junior department won not only the circuit shield, but also every award in the Leeds District. Alas, the rules stipulated that they were only allowed to receive one title.

John Wesley's preaching must have had a major influence in Wakefield, for many chapels sprang up in both town and country. Mrs Abson notes that 'at Lee Moor, a Wesleyan Methodist Society was formed over 200 years ago.' The Society must have flourished, for in 1801 they built the Wesleyan Methodist Chapel in the village on the site of the cock-pit. It was said this was an instance of God triumphant over the Devil. The building was nearly square and was possibly built of stone from the nearby quarry. Inside a gallery ran round three sides and the simple little pulpit had come from Thornhill Street Chapel, Wakefield, in 1803. John Wesley is said to have preached from this pulpit when it was at Thornhill Street. A stable for the horses of visiting preachers was attached to the chapel. The chapel and Sunday school, which met in the same building until 1926, had a strong religious and musical influence on the village for many generations, and for a long period it was a hive of activity. Many a backslider still treasures the Sunday school prizes received for good attendance and remembers the hymns and some of the lessons he heard along with the names of his teachers.

Opposite: *Brunswick Methodist Church, Saville Street. This building was opened in 1876 and closed in 1985. The first church was built in 1865 at the personal expense of George William Harrison, the foundation stones being laid by the mayor of Wakefield, Mr W.H. Lee. This building was situated in Lower York Street, and would figure, as the Wakefield Academy, in the lives of many of Wakefield's leading citizens. The school did yeoman service until funds were raised to build a proper church capable of accommodating 650 of the faithful. Frederick Simpson, a Wakefield architect, drew up plans enabling additional seating for up to 900, by the creation of a gallery. The society only had forty-three members at the time, and was being overly optimistic. The new church, called Brunswick, was opened on 11 July 1876. It was not until the Revd E. Boocock came to Brunswick that the society expanded. The Revd E. Dunstan was its most noted minister. During the Second World War, the school was used as an evacuation centre. The society celebrated its centenary in 1976. Brunswick was closed in 1985 to become part of the present day Trinity Methodist Church on Norton Road.*

Grove Methodist Church. The first chapel of the Methodist New Connexion was opened in Wakefield in 1821 and was situated in Crown Court. The congregation moved from this building to Grove Road in 1866. Grove Road closed in 1978 and merged with Eastmoor Methodists. Admiral C.H. Binstead was an active supporter of the church, and would often provide free or discounted tickets for travel on the Lancashire & Yorkshire Railway, of which he was passenger superintendent. These were for the chapel for outings to the coast. In 1899 the chapel was remodelled and the present entrance was built. The rebuilding of the tower and spire was completed in 1904, as the original structure was deemed unsafe. However, the 1904 spire was removed in 1975, despite much protest by the Wakefield Historical Society.

In 1953, a new organ by Wood Wordsworth & Co. of Leeds was installed. This instrument was enlarged in 1960 when funds had been raised to allow three stops, recovered from the organ at Bethel, to be installed. The centenary was celebrated in 1966, the same year that West Parade was merged with Grove Road. Desiring a single city centre chapel, Grove Road was closed in 1978, and the members moved to the chapel at Eastmoor. The organ was moved to Castleford United Reformed Church. The building is today partly restored, but will likely be converted into housing, having stood empty since 1979.

At Alverthorpe the public teas acquired something of a reputation. The sisterhood withstood many vicissitudes but still kept going. The Sunday school premises were used for many years as a child welfare clinic. Up to the Second World War, there was a young ladies' class and a young men's class in existence and many a match had been made under their auspices!

While spiritual needs were looked after, bodily fitness was not forgotten; a punch ball, chest expanders and Indian clubs were part of the chapel's sports equipment; two football teams were at one time playing regularly every Saturday afternoon. There was also a mid-week games class, with table tennis, darts and dominoes. One vividly recalls fetching a billiards table from a house in Southgate on a lorry, belonging to Mr Alf Hessary and singing all the way home for sheer joy at having acquired such a treasure. In quieter mood there was a drawing class for boys and a sewing class for the girls.

In the 1950s, there were the pantomimes; the authentic one with Mrs Barlow in charge as producer, and the not-so-authentic ones by the men of the church (never really sure whether they had a producer or not). Cinderella's coach was made from an old pram body for one of this latter category. Other churches also had pantomimes, a large production usually taking place for the circuit every year at Wesley Hall.

The Sunday school treats were wonderful occasions, with the teachers starting early to make up the bags of buns and weighing out screws of Yorkshire Mixtures from Talbot's Sweet Factory in Flanshaw Lane. In the early afternoon there was the assembling outside, eagerly awaiting the arrival of Mr Jack Cuthbert with his horse and cart; the man-handling into position of the harmonium

Pantomime at Wesley Hall Methodist Church, Horbury Road, c. *1937.*

and anchoring it down with ropes, then with Joe Lindley at the keyboard around the village, singing the anniversary hymns.

Tea was served and then all went to Silcoates field for games and competitions. In the late evening, a tired company would assemble in Silcoates College grounds and sing to the assembled students. Three cheers from us to them and three from them to us, and a perfect end to another School Anniversary.

Gilbert Brummitt

Bethel Methodists, Thornes Lane. The first Methodist chapel in Thornes was opened in 1832 and was unique in having been formerly a converted coal barge moored at Thornes Wharf. The boat had belonged to Jimmy Hirst of Rawcliffe. The chapel was described as a timber gothic structure built on the deck of the boat, and fitted up with pews, pulpit and a small pipe organ. By 1853, the old boat was leaking so badly that during the services the boat keeper had to keep pumping the water out. Alternative accommodation was found at Salem Congregational Church. The Revd J.S. Eastmead, the minister at Salem, who would be described as ecumenical today, allowed his church to be used by other nonconformist societies.

George William Harrison saw the need for a proper church building and provided a new structure at his own expense. The ministers of Salem Congregational Chapel and Market Street United Methodist Free Church led the services on alternate Sundays, but, at Mr Harrison's request, the Congregationalists withdrew. The society quickly outgrew their home, and the foundations of the current building were laid on 21 May 1870, and opened, ten months later, on 23 March 1871. Bad winter weather in the immediate post war years, and a greatly reduced congregation, led to the closure of the church on 31 March 1952. The organ's pine panelling was moved to Grove Road Methodist Church, by the young men's group run by Eric Swinden, and made into two vestry screens.

Market Street United Methodists. A number of Wesleyan Methodists broke away, in 1849, to form the United Methodist Free Church. West Parade and other chapels in the area were disgruntled at the way the church was being run by a national body. The founder of the movement, Revd James Everett, held the first services at Salem Congregational Church on George Street, and had 1,000 members from the movement's inception. Mr W. Shaw of Stanley Hall, who was also a trustee, along with Mr George William Harrison, the first mayor of Wakefield, laid the foundation stone of the present Market Street church on 2 February 1858. Other notables in the congregation were organ builder Francis Booth and a young George Crook, who became a notable architect. The union of Methodists in 1932 made both Market Street chapels surplus to requirements, and plans were made to merge all city centre chapels with West Parade. Market Street United Methodists was closed on 28 July 1935, and the building was sold to the General Post Office for £2,100. Today the building is the Grand Central Diner.

WHITSUNTIDE AND CHRISTMAS

One of the most enjoyable leisure time activities associated with either church or chapel, and one which played an important part in the whole town and nearby villages, was that of music making. Almost everyone, from all age groups, took part in one way or another. The majority of the children of Wakefield and surrounding areas were taught hymns at a very early age in church and Methodist Sunday schools. Many people remember singing as being a notable feature of village and town life, especially on the occasions of Sunday school anniversaries and Whitsuntide, when children paraded through the town. Singing their special hymns they would parade to Thornes Park or other similar open spaces.

A Whitsun outing to a local park, mid-1930s.

A picnic lunch was served on trestle tables.

After the picnic, games were held. Here we see Sunday school teachers bobbing for apples.

The junior members of the Sunday school enjoying a game.

West Parade Methodist Church badminton club, c. *1928.*

A way of raising funds was to hold a sale of work. This one is taking place in the Sunday school of West Parade Methodist Church, c. *1925. Judging by the items on sale, needlepoint was a very popular pastime.*

By this time, the West Riding Bus Company had introduced the first solid tyre buses for transport and one of the early choir trips was to Buxton and Bakewell, using two buses and had been organised by Mr Swinden's father Lawrence, and Charlie Wrigglesworth.

Many hymns were sung during the journey and the popular song of the day was 'Tiptoe through the Tulips'. At one stage, after the men had played bowls at Buxton, the party halted by the roadside when a large lorry discharged Walls ices, much to the delight of all passengers on a warm day.

The minister at Westgate Wesleyans at the time was the Revd Frank Boynton, who was one of the first people among the congregation at Westgate End I knew to have his own transport – an Austin 7 Saloon, then valued at £120. The annual Whitsunday treat for the children was organised by a strong band of teachers led by a very efficient Sunday school secretary, Edith M. Cameron, who was the daughter of J.C. Cameron, one of the principal movers in the building of the New School, and who was the proprietor of the general grocer's shop and bakery in New Scarborough, which was always a great advantage when eating events were being arranged. She had to cater for over 100 scholars and their parents. All travelled by two electric trams from Lawfield Lane End

/continued overleaf

West Parade Methodist Church's Sunday school Whitsuntide treat, c. 1930. The scholars gather outside the school.

/continued from previous page

through the centre of Wakefield to the Sandal Terminus discharging their children and teachers to run the length of Walton Lane to Sellers Farm.

Meals had been carefully prepared in the morning by the teachers and packed into large baskets supplied by Messrs Hayleys Worsted Spinners and loaded, along with trestle forms, on to a Beverley's brewer

lorry. Edgar Swinden, who was transport manager at Beverley's, drove it to Walton. Later the minister concluded that the brewery lorry should not be used for a Methodist function and forbade it, whereupon Edgar Swinden never went to the chapel again.

As the trams proceeded to Walton the children sang hymns and popular songs to the listening pedestrians, as there were few private cars on the road at that time. Before the Sunday school feast ended, all children and parents gathered together on the grass to sing anniversary hymns.

Christmas also followed a regular pattern for most of the churches and chapels in Wakefield, with special carol singing for Christmas Eve. At Westgate End those participating had first to attend, for two or three weeks, after evening

Dressing the Christmas tree, c. 1935.

service, to learn part-singing under the baton and tuning fork of Eric Bradley. Part-singing was essential as the carol party sang their way around the houses of the congregation from 8 p.m. to 6 a.m., taking a short break about midnight for hot refreshment prepared by the caretaker at the Sunday school.

In the early afternoon there was the assembling outside the chapel, and eagerly awaiting the arrival of Mr Jack Cuthbert with his horse and cart; the manhandling into position of the harmonium and anchoring it down with ropes, then, with Joe Lindley at the keyboard, the whole school processed around Alverthorpe, singing the hymns and carols. Every chapel in the circuit held similar functions at Whitsuntide and for the anniversary. In the late evening, a tired company would assemble in Silcoates College grounds and sing to the assembled students.

Gilbert Brummitt

Proceeds from the resultant collection on Christmas morning was used to finance the Sunday school Christmas parties, which were always concluded by each child receiving an apple and orange as they went home. The efficient Sunday school secretary organised the well-disciplined tea and games, which followed. Parents were always delighted with the arrangements.

Ron Swinden

Westgate End chapel's outing to Buxton, 1930s.

The Dewsbury Road Methodist Church proudly opened a new Sunday school on Saturday 29 June 1963. Sadly the building has since been demolished.

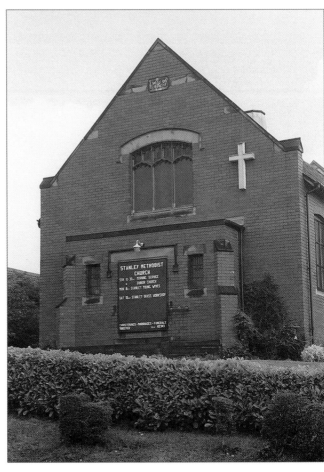

Stanley Methodist church. The Primitive Methodists opened the first chapel in 1841, with a new building being built in 1876. This remained in use until the early 1970s, when the congregation moved into the 1929 Sunday school of Stanley Wesleyan Methodist church on Mount Road, which had closed in the mid-1960s.

*Lakeside Chapel,
Newmillerdam, 1890.
The chapel, which
stands to this day,
replaced an earlier one
built in the 1820s on
School Hill.*

*Woodmoor Chapel,
Newmillerdam, 2003.*

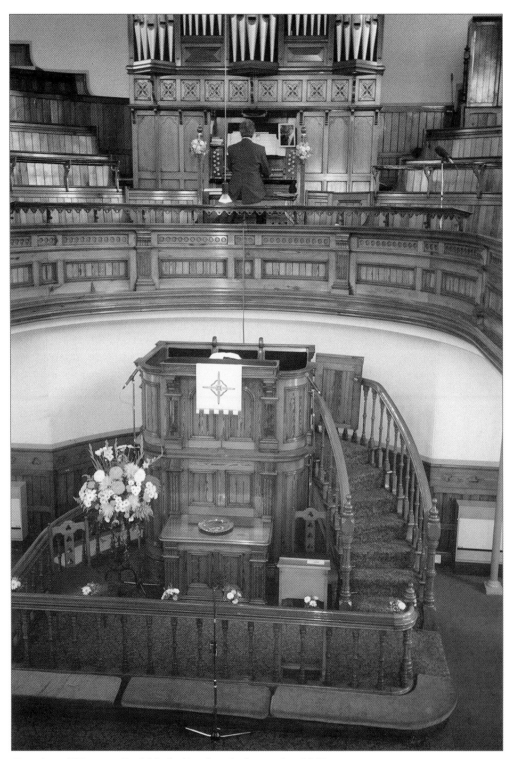

Interior of Westgate End Methodist church, September 1993.

ANGLICAN CHURCHES

In Wakefield, there was always a sense of rivalry between the choirs of the different churches and chapels. The Anglican Cathedral of All Saints always wanted to maintain its high musical standard, and therefore wanted the best choir in the city. Thus, the head chorister at Holy Trinity church on George Street found himself singing in the cathedral rather than in his parish church. The chorister was a young Kenneth Leighton, who would become a nationally important composer. He was thereafter associated with the cathedral: something for which Holy Trinity never forgave the cathedral.

St Mary's, on Primrose Hill, was a large stone building with a spire that grew out of the top of the tower. It was a better-looking church than St Andrew's, and had a wonderful encaustic tile floor in the chancel and choir. It was built by the church commissioners from money given to England after the battle of Waterloo, but was not a million-fund church like St James's, Thornes or St Peter's, Stanley. The church had no organist during the war, so my friend at school, Dorothy Chatfield, asked me if I could play for some services. Her father was the vicar at St Mary's. The organ had three manuals. It was a very cold church. I was a pianist and not an organist. I played occasionally midweek but never on a Sunday, as I would attend chapel with my parents at Westgate End. St Mary's was closed down in the early 1960s and merged with St Andrew's. The pulpit was moved to St Andrew's, as was the altar.

St Andrew's was built by George Gilbert Scott, but was never quite finished. On the front is a large blocked-in arch where the tower was meant to go: money presumably ran out. The church had a remarkably ugly font that would certainly make any baby cry.

Another small church which survived for some time was at the bottom of the grammar school playing fields. It was a typical tin tab. It looked more like a sports pavilion, associated with the sports club nearby, or the grammar school, than a church. It was called St Mark's, and it closed in the late 1970s.

Jeane Cresswell

Holy Trinity church, George Street. This centre of worship, opened in the 1840s, was for a long time a far more fashionable church than the cathedral. In fact, on nearby South Parade, the rooms to the front of the houses were in the parish of Holy Trinity, and the rooms to the rear in the parish of All Saints. One of the greatest Victorian hymn writers was associated with the church – the Revd J.B. Dykes. Dykes was a close friend of Francis Booth and his brother was a bank manager in Wakefield, living on South Parade; both Dykes and Booth would often play the organ. The church was very evangelical. The dispersal of the population from the city centre to new council estates meant the dwindling of the congregation. This diaspora was so severe that the church was closed in 1954, and demolished soon after.

St John's Church (right) *was built in 1791 as a chapel of ease to the parish church. The building of the church was proposed in 1723, but opposition from the vicar of Wakefield terminated the scheme. The church was designed as the centrepiece of John Lee's new town, called St John's. The original building was extended with the construction of the current chancel in 1905. The tower dates from 1895, when the original was damaged by a lightning strike.*

The foundation stones of the small Georgian church, St James's (below right), *were laid on 6 August 1829 by Mr James Milnes. The building of the church was funded by the 'Million Fund' and Mr and Mrs Gaskell. In the early 1950s with the closure of Christ Church* (below left), *St James's became St James's and Christ Church.*

The church has always had a fine musical tradition. As Mr Ronald Pearson notes:

'The family returned to Wakefield (1919) and we came to live in an old cottage (since demolished) in Holmfield Lane, Thornes. It was at this time that I became a choirboy at St James's church, Thornes. Mr Thomas Clarkson was the organist and choirmaster, and I

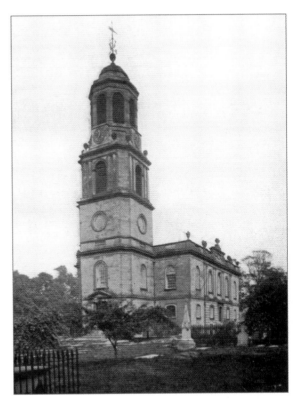

remained a member until my voice broke. It used to be said that Thornes church would never be short of choirboys, for most of the Thornes boys had sung before the Queen, the Bishop and the Admiral.

The Queen's Arms and the Bishop Blaize were public houses in Thornes, and the Admiral Duncan in Thornes Lane.

After the First World War, new churches were built to cater for the new suburban housing estates. In the 1920s the Lupset housing estate was built, and new places of worship were opened. First was Wesley Hall Wesleyan church on Thornes Road, the Dewsbury Road Primitive Methodists and then St George's Anglican parish church. The foundations of our new church were laid by Bishop Eden in 1928.

It was built by George Crook and Sons, who had built Snapethorpe School, where I would become a teacher. Mr Crook was a member of Market Street 'Victoria' Methodist Church, not 'Ebenezer', which became the Queen Street Hall. St George's was finally opened in 1935. The plans showed the church to have a spire and tower, but due to lack of funds it was never completed.

Ruth Tetley

CHRIST CHURCH, THORNES

The vicar of Thornes, Revd Henry Jones of St James's, was distressed by the apparent purloining of his congregation and had to consider whether to enlarge his building or to build a new church to accommodate more people and extend the influence of the established church in the area. Canon Wyndham Mason Maddon BA of Holy Trinity Church, however, leant towards the latter option, believing that the people of Thornes would benefit from a new church. To this effect, Mrs Robinson, the wife of Revd Disney Robinson of Woolley, offered, at her own expense, to erect 'a large and beautiful church' for the people of Thornes. She also offered to endow it and provide a parsonage for the vicar and a mission hall, on the condition that the sitting committee would undertake to provide the required amount for the remainder of the buildings necessary to form a complete church organisation. Mrs Robinson donated the princely sum of £8,650. The Bishop of Ripon opened the new church on 22 April 1876.

ROMAN CATHOLIC CHURCH

ST AUSTIN'S

St Austin's was built in 1826 to the designs of W.C. Hansom, the inventor of the hansom cab. It is Wakefield's only Catholic church.

May Day processions, that was in the days when the parishioners walked through the streets of Wakefield, when the girls all wore long white dresses with wreaths of flowers in their hair; some had white flowers, some red and some yellow. These were to represent the joyful, sorrowful and glorious mysteries of the rosary. The girls were followed by a large contingent of boy scouts and cubs with the women and the men bringing up the rear. The May procession was a very happy occasion and, looking back, it must have been a great witness to the people of Wakefield. The people would gather in church prior to the start of the procession and begin singing hymns. The procession would then begin heading down Wood Street, around the Bull Ring and returning down Northgate. On other occasions the procession would head down Northgate towards Newton Bar, cut across St John's North and then head back to church.

It is quite amazing when we start looking at old photos how so many wonderful memories of the past which seem to have been forgotten come vividly back to life again. One of those memories is our adoration of the Blessed Sacrament. Who remembers the forty-hour devotions we had in those days? The altar would be adorned with lovely flowers and brilliant with candles. The beauty, silence and peace of the atmosphere seemed to make one so aware of the holiness, transcendence and yes the very nearness of God and, if I remember rightly, there was never any shortage of people to keep vigil even during the night. The forty-hour devotion was a special time of prayer for the entire parish, from which we all derived great benefit; perhaps in those days we were all more acutely aware of our need of God. Another regular devotion was Sunday evening devotion at 6.30 p.m.: Rosary, sermon and Benediction. Of course that was before we had evening mass. One of the hymns I remember so vividly from those days is the one written by St Bernard:

> Jesu, the very thought of thee
> with sweetness fills my breast;
> but sweeter far thy face to see.
> and in thy presence rest.
>
> Nor voice can sing, nor heart can frame,
> nor can the memory find
> a sweeter sound than thy blest name,
> O Saviour of mankind.

O hope of every contrite heart,
O joy of all the meek;
to those who fall, how kind thou art,
how good to those who seek!

But what to those who find? Ah, this
nor tongue nor pen can show;
the love of Jesus, what it is
none but his lovers know.

Jesu, our only joy be thou,
as thou our prize wilt be;
Jesu, be thou our glory now,
and through eternity.

Words: attributed to Bernard of Clairvaux (1091–1153)
translated by Edward Caswall (1814–78)
Music: A. Edmunds Tozer (1857–1910)

Yes, a wealth of treasured memories, and one more memory of devotion to the blessed sacrament is the memorable celebration of the feast of Corpus Christi, when the blessed sacrament was carried solemnly under the special canopy around the church accompanied by the ringing of bells and the singing of *Pange Lingua Gloriosi* and a procession of young boys walking backwards before the blessed sacrament, strewing rose petals; these petals afterwards would be picked up by parishioners and reverently kept in one's prayer book.

Of course in those days the church, like most of the rest of us, was poor in material wealth. There were no carpets on the floor, just wooden planks. These were scrubbed once a year – the Tuesday evening of Holy Week. To begin with the wood was dry and absolutely black, engrained with the dirt and grime of a whole year of being trampled on. It literally took buckets and buckets of hot water to make any impression at all; but we scrubbed and scrubbed and gradually one would begin to see the original colour of the wood shining through, and by the end of the night what a transformation had taken place; it was with pride and satisfaction we viewed our efforts as the church just gleamed in its freshness and cleanness, all ready for the great feast of Easter. The evening's work was always followed by a very enjoyable fish and chip supper down in the rooms provided by dear Monsignor Thompson.

Julie Burke

St Austin's, like the Methodists and the Church of England, had its own school. A former pupil describes her memories of St Austin's School:

I was born in Grove House, Grove Road, down Kirkgate, in July 1926. Baptised at St Austin's in August and then taken a week later to the convent in Teal Street to be dedicated to Our Lady.

In the year 1931, I was sent to Wakefield from Lupset estate to a Catholic school. The journey forth and back is firmly etched in my memory. I would leave my home at 12 Milton Crescent, the other side of Snapethorp school, and walk up Broadway and down to Horbury Road to catch a tram or bus to the Bull Ring. The fare was a halfpenny. When arriving in the Bull Ring I would cross traffic to New Street and walk through rows of old terrace houses, past the slaughterhouse where the bleating of doomed sheep was the daily signal that around the corner was my destination: St Austin's.

It was a dreary building on the outside, black from years of coal and soot, very much an ancient relic of the past even then. Upon entering to find one's room I would bump into others arriving, literally, as it was so hard to adjust your eyes to the darkness of the inside. There was an electric light bulb hanging from the ceiling, but I am sure now, looking back, the wattage must have been around forty amps.

The bright spot in this whole scenario was Sister Patrick; she was our first teacher, old, plump and kindly and had taught my father before me, so I was well received. The aroma was very distinctive; it was a mixture of dry bread, jam, dripping and soggy newspaper.

When all were announced present and correct, and all prayers said, Sister Patrick collected all the dinners the children had brought and they all were deposited in a wicker basket by her side on the floor – the source of the constant aroma. At noon after the angelus bell was rung we were allowed to gather a dinner from the basket and eat it in the school. My cousin, Terry Clarke, who started school the same day, and I were very fortunate to carry our lunches in tiny suitcases and they remained intact once we arrived at school. Sometimes we were accosted by boys much older, who were well known for bullying, and they would look in our suitcases for fruit, which they would take. Remember those were very hard times for lots of people in Yorkshire and there were lots of people on the dole and many a time the children would gather around me if I did have a apple for playtime and each would beg the core or 'conk' as they called it. They are the ones who could tell some stories if we could find them.

/continued overleaf

/continued from previous page

During the first year I remember the first school concert that I was in. There was a little girl who was very pretty. Her last name I think was Cairns. She was chosen to be the fairy princess, all in white and silver, but the wise Sister Patrick chose other girls to be fairies also and I was the 'lavender fairy in purple and green, the prettiest fairy ever was seen'. That was my introductory line to the following years of school concerts. And we were brought back on a certain Saturday afternoon for a dress rehearsal and I dropped my wand down a grate in the playground.

The year passed. Pictures were taken in front of the convent, and I moved up into Miss Rainer's class and felt quite old and experienced in contrast to the wee ones entering Sister Patrick's room after the summer holidays. Miss Rainer was a young teacher and taught us well but I don't have any recollection of any outstanding details except another picture was taken in the same spot. All the photos were staged in front of the convent with a bit of green privet for a backdrop.

In those days the toilets were outside and bits of newspaper on a string were there for our use. Hygiene was not invented so there was no washing of hands during the school day. My mother called for me a few times after her market shopping was completed, usually on a Friday when I had to go for new shoes, or when it was close to Whitsuntide to be outfitted with new clothes. Otherwise I never remember anyone accompanying me to school even from the first day. Looking back I find this whole episode quite remarkable, especially in light of the present day. With motor cars not yet widely available, people made entertainment where they could and St Austin's became a centre for socialising. Families would meet regularly in the church rooms for dancing and various games. Sunday evening, following Benediction in the afternoon, was a favourite time for socialising.

Eileen Little

4

Wartime Wakefield

Britain had feared air attack, even before the war, and, from 1938, had set up a voluntary defence organisation called Air Raid Precautions (ARP: later called Civil Defence). This was designed to give help to the people during and after air raids with high-explosive bombs, incendiaries (fire-bombs) and poison gas.

Over 2,500 Wakefield people served in the city's ARP as rescue, ambulance or first aid workers, emergency feeding teams and air raid wardens (who helped the people in each street to find shelter when the sirens sounded). Very important also were the Auxiliary Fire Service (helping the fire brigade) and the special constables (helping the police). Many ARP workers did this work on top of their normal jobs.

The primary German target in Wakefield was the railway, because a huge amount of war material and troops were moved through the city by this means. One railway target was Charles Roberts's railway wagon works at Horbury Junction.

Even before the war, the Germans had gathered maps and photos of their targets. There are copies of the German target maps for Wakefield, and some of the target photographs, in Wakefield's local studies library. Because everyone took shelter when there was an air raid, incendiary bombs could start a large fire unnoticed. Volunteer fire watchers were stationed on the top of tall buildings at nights (when air raids were most predominant). They kept a lookout for fires, and put them out if possible, or called the fire services. The work was often cold and uncomfortable, and could be dangerous – the Germans deliberately added explosives to some of their incendiary bombs in order to kill fire fighters.

More than 1 in 10 of the bombs dropped did not explode – they were either operated with a delayed-action timer fuse, or were faulty. It was the job of bomb disposal teams to dig out unexploded bombs and defuse them. This was especially dangerous work because the bomb fuses were often booby-trapped. Wakefield's bomb disposal team was a unit of the Royal Engineers based here at Alverthorpe Hall. This unit defused two huge bombs dropped in December 1940, but one in the yard of Wakefield Prison and one at Chantry Lane, Lupset, were only discovered weeks later.

The first air attack on Wakefield was on 28 August 1940 by a single German bomber. At 1.45 a.m. it dropped a high explosive bomb which destroyed four houses in Norton Street, Belle Vue, and damaged many more. The police report of the raid, in Wakefield's local studies library, lists one woman and three men injured, ranging in age from seventeen to eighty-three years old; they were taken to Clayton

The Lupset bomb.

Hospital, while many others were given first aid on the spot. Although the damage was to a civilian area, these houses were only 400 yards from important railway and industrial targets, including Wakefield's main petrol storage, which was just across the canal. If the bombs had been released only five seconds later, the result would have been a major disaster. Further small raids followed, and sadly, on 1 September 1940 at Wragby, a delayed-action bomb, dropped on the previous night, exploded, killing seven, mainly ARP workers, and injuring a policeman.

A fortnight later, in the early evening of 16 September 1940, ten high explosive and forty incendiary bombs fell over the area from Clarence Park through Thornes Wharf to Barnsley Road, but most landed in open ground. One house, near Busy Corner on Barnsley Road, was demolished; one fireman was injured, but otherwise only a parrot in the house was killed.

In December 1940, three high explosive and twenty incendiary bombs fell on Wakefield. Bombers that had overshot their target – in all likelihood, Sheffield – probably dropped these. Craters found at Chantry Lane, Lupset and in the prison yard were thought to be the result of small bombs that had already exploded. Weeks later the bomb disposal team from Alverthorpe Hall examined the craters more closely, and discovered unexploded bombs that had penetrated deep into the ground. The Royal Engineers dug out these huge bombs – each one weighed a ton and a half – and made them safe in February and March 1941 respectively. On the night of 14/15 March 1941, Sheffield was once again the target for a significant part of the German bomber force. However, unlike the raids in December 1940, the Sheffield attack was not this time led by the expert German Pathfinder crews (who used radio beams to navigate accurately). As a result, many of the German aircraft lost their way and attacked Leeds, Castleford and Wakefield among other places.

At 10.53 p.m. two large high explosive bombs fell on Thornes Road, killing five people – two children, a woman and two men – and injuring five more, one of whom later died of the wounds. Six houses were demolished -- including the one in this photograph – and over 200 were damaged. The ages of the dead ranged from two to eighty years old. Wakefield was fortunate that a large bomb dropped by parachute (a land-mine) was caught by the wind and blown away from the town centre, finally exploding at Wrenthorpe, where it badly damaged a single house.

During the Second World War, many foods and other goods were unobtainable or were strictly rationed. For example, the supply of many imported foods such as bananas and oranges dried up, and almost all meat was rationed. The shopper had to produce a ration book with coupons that allowed them to buy a set amount of meat, butter, or sugar, each week. People were encouraged to grow their own vegetables on allotments. The rationing system continued in use for certain types of foods, such as sugar and sweets, long after the war was over.

A street with blacked-out road sign, somewhere on the Lupset estate, c. 1943.

Every effort was made to recycle metal, paper, and other scarce items such as rubber, to help towards the war effort. Each item recycled meant that space was saved in the convoys of ships bringing supplies to Britain across the North Atlantic from America. German submarines frequently attacked these ships, and many merchantmen were sunk. Salvage drives were a regular feature of wartime life, when everything from old pots and pans to newspaper and iron railings were collected.

Wakefield's last air raid was on the morning of Christmas Eve 1944, when a fleet of forty-five German bombers, over the North Sea near Spurn Head, launched flying bombs – an early type of cruise missile (called V1s by the Germans and buzz-bombs or doodlebugs by the British). These were aimed at Manchester, but almost all crashed before they reached their target. One came down on farmland at Grange Moor, blasting a large crater, but causing little damage.

BUILD-UP TO WAR

By 1938 there was a real fear of war, and a collection was made at school (Wakefield Girls High School) for Czechoslovakian refugees. But, despite the international situation, Miss Maris took a party of girls to Switzerland.

August for an eleven-year-old appears to have been a string of hot days spent cycling to Coxley Valley for picnics, swimming and playing tennis.

Parents spent much time, as many would later, listening to the news bulletins and talking about the German invasion of Poland and the Baltic area; Danzig and the corridor were a major worry. All at school were advised by Miss Maris to carry on quietly in school and with their own business in as normal a way as possible. The Friday night (1 September) was spent lying with her sister and friends on the lawn of the family home watching a lone single-engined plane fly over, which had to be a Spitfire even then. The last minutes of peace were ticking away.

From then on the excitement rose, but parents became sadder and more resolute. They remembered and had fought in the First World War, the 'war to end all wars', their memories were horrendous – and now it was happening again. 'Twenty years' was repeated again and again. The family had no sons, but had cousins who were of an age to go and fight. Indeed one, Eric Bradley, had been called up with the militia twelve months earlier. The Saturday passed and nothing. No chapel on the Sunday morning added to the gloomy atmosphere of suspense.

The wireless was turned on about 10:50 a.m. and all sat down to wait out the last few minutes, an experience that many do not want to repeat. Then Neville Chamberlain's serious voice came on the wireless telling us and the world that the last hour of the ultimatum had passed and that we were therefore at war with Germany and her allies. Life for many seemed to stop that day as though no one knew what to do next. In a way the news was a relief. The war began less with a bang than a whimper of apprehension.

The blackout had come, and we were told that, in the event of an air raid, we must go under the table – a large sturdy oak affair – or under the piano – a boudoir grand with enormous legs. Later, the cellar was emptied out and the marble slabs were equipped with blankets and pillows, reminiscent of a morgue.

That night the air raid siren sounded nearly all over Britain, but it did not last long. An elderly aunt, Ruth Harvey, lived with her mother, Alice Harvey, on Dewsbury Road, and during the raid one of her neighbours went to see that she was all right, only to be very startled by just her head appearing round the door in its gas mask.

Jeane Cresswell

The mayor and some of Wakefield's servicemen, 1943.

SCHOOL

Autumn term at school started again in the second week of September, on the 14th, to find that the greatest sin on the calendar was not having your gas mask with you at all times. For a while every lesson began with a gas mask check. Later it became a registration ceremony, which lasted until the last days of the war. If you had forgotten it, you were sent home to retrieve it. Gas mask drills – putting them on, chin first and the straps over your head, staff in theirs checking straps. They smelt horrible. Puffing and blowing to see that you had a good seal, moving around a little to get used to wearing them, became part of the timetable. Miss Frampton was always meticulous. Sticky white paper criss-crossed the windows to prevent flying glass.

Air raid drills, when we were asked to get our gas masks, became a welcome timetable break; all had to line up at the door with their gas mask and walk quietly to the school's cellar, which eventually had benches to sit on. Those who did not have a cellar peg had to use the corridors, boiler rooms and storage areas of the school. The pupils went in to the cellar in lesson divisions, full forms for humanities and for sciences, languages and mathematics groups consisting of roughly one third of each of the two parallel forms. The relevant member of staff would take the register of the group she had been teaching. This all became, as intended, routine, but at first there were some girls at the school who would become hysterical, but received little sympathy. The cellar had numerous pipes crossing it and the staff were worried about their fracturing in the event of the school being hit. If the girls were in the cellar during an air raid, and the gas and hot water pipes were broken, there could have been a disaster.

Once the initial excitement had died down, all these things became a matter of routine, and were never carried out in anger. Life settled down to normal. For an eleven-year-old sitting in class, and daily watching the flags move around a map of Europe, the war virtually died until Dunkirk came and the Battle of Britain started.

At the Girls High School, fire watching was organised. Each night two members of staff and two members of the sixth form would be on duty. Later on, everyone over sixteen did fire watching, which involved sleeping at the school about once a month, making coffee for the staff on duty and actually sitting in the staff common room when homework was finished. Everyone did their turn of fire watching at their office or factory. An incendiary bomb could be easily put out if someone was there to raise the alarm. An unwatched building may well be alight before an alarm was sounded. There were alarms at night and air raid warnings but fortunately none were near to Wentworth House. The watchers were either left listening to eerie cracks and groans of the empty school or trying to sleep, the girls in a lecture room, the staff in the staff room or any corner which was more convenient. In the raid on Thornes Road, one of the girl's homes was damaged but not destroyed.

School activities had to be curtailed because of the war, and primarily because of the blackout. In the spring term of 1940 a lecture was given by the Society for the Propagation of the Gospel and the only event was the hockey team party. The dinner was shortened so that the girls could get home before dark. The bus services were irregular, and the journey home could be an ordeal if there was no bus. As much as possible was fitted into the shortened dinner hour: choir practice, discussion groups, Guide meetings, and working parties.

There were fewer journeys for many outside school, but entertainment came to school instead. In 1942, two concerts were given by the Northern Philharmonia Orchestra in the Jubilee Hall, and 110 girls went to see the London Philharmonic at the Unity Hall. In February 1942, the women of the ATS gave a marching display in Jubilee Hall. As the war progressed, school activities went back to normal, though there still was no dramatic competition or sports day.

Jeane Cresswell

During the First World War, part of the High School was made into a military hospital. It was then that the wooden teaching rooms, known to many old girls of the school as the huts, were built to accommodate the girls, because many of the form rooms were made into wards, which were named after the famous generals of the time, such as French, Haig, Kitchener. The names stayed painted over the doors until the late 1940s, and the huts remained until the 1960s. A major drawback with the way in which the huts were planned was that the only way to get from one to the other was through another hut. All the huts opened off one another, so the

/continued on next page

/continued from previous page

only way to reach the middle hut was via the gymnasium and then through either huts 1 or 2 or in by the Margaret Street door. This meant that if a girl or teacher was late for lessons, they would disturb the entire block of huts getting to their class. On a wet day you had to walk through all five to the reach the end one. Miss Benson had tramlines painted on the floor, and depending on which way you walked depended on which tramline you took. Indeed some girls were allowed out of class early to catch their buses home, and they caused even more disturbance by bidding good afternoon to all members of staff as they passed through the huts.

Shirley Murdock

The mayor and some of Wakefield's servicemen and women, 1943.

In place of the school trips and outings, some girls went each year to a harvest camp. In 1941 it was fruit picking in Huntingdonshire. In 1943 school was closed for a week in October while a party of V Uppers and VI Uppers went to camp. The V Lowers and VI Lowers had been the previous week, so got their holidays at the expense of the Uppers. The work was either picking potatoes or pulling sugar beet. The girls slept on palliasses and got up at six in the morning, and still enjoyed the recreations of tennis, table tennis, dancing and walking. Another group at the same camp at Walton near Boston Spa, Lincolnshire, forgot to get up in the morning to go to work. The last camp took place in October 1945.

Jeane Cresswell

CHURCH AND CHAPEL

The years 1938/9 were tense times for all as Britain lurched from one crisis to another during Chamberlain's efforts to appease Mussolini and Hitler, and soon the young men of the chapel were being registered for National Service. Initially Douglas Wright and Eric Bradley were mobilised, but later when war broke out there was a succession of young people and teachers being called to the forces. Alice Dunnill, now Roberts, took the lead in obtaining comforts and money to send to the lads away from home.

The outbreak of the Second World War created new problems, and at Westgate End they received a call from the city council for churches to send delegates to an inaugural meeting to establish youth activities for those leaving school. Miss Crawford was appointed to set up the first city youth club, and Westgate End was one of the first Methodist societies to become involved as a Methodist Youth Fellowship. Two other well-supported clubs were also launched, Lupset St George's and Eastmoor Popular. Certain food rations were made available to organised bodies, and, although lacking members, Westgate End organised a cricket match against Eastmoor Popular, which Leslie Jacques won almost single-handed with both bat and ball.

Obviously with many men and lads away, chapel and Sunday school members declined, but it was proud to boast that throughout the war regular activities at Westgate End continued even to the extent of carol singing as before. One result of the war,

/continued overleaf

/continued from previous page

due to blackouts, was that evening services were replaced by afternoon. Fortunately other Methodist societies recognised this gap with Dewsbury Road and Wesley Hall arranging singsongs, mostly for the young.

During the war, some chapels were closed entirely. At Thorpe-on-the-Hill, the small ex-Wesleyan chapel was closed, and the congregation met at Lofthouse Chapel. At Oulton the big ex-Wesleyan chapel was shut. Of course this may have also been due to circuit rationalisation after unification in 1932, but Thorpe at least re-opened. Many Sunday school buildings and halls were hired to the army or council. Alverthorpe, Wesley Hall, Brunswick and certainly others had rooms commandeered for government use. They were mainly welfare centres for young children, and the old.

Ron Swinden

Sun Lane swimming baths were used during the war to train Royal Marine divers. Here we see deputy mayor Councillor H. Watson talking to some of the divers.

Due to the blackout restrictions, it was very difficult to black out all the windows in the chapel, and coupled with the expense of trying to heat two large buildings, the chapel and Sunday school, and the restrictions on fuel, the chapel was seldom used, and, especially during the winter months, the Sunday school was used as both chapel and school. The chapel met in the large assembly hall. During the summer the chapel would be used, as it was warmer and lighter, but evening services would be held in the Sunday school, as it was easier to black out.

When Belle Vue was bombed, the chapel on Doncaster Road was damaged, as the bomb fell about 50 yards away on Dunbar Street/Norton Street, which went down the side of the chapel.

Shirley Murdock

The outbreak of war in September 1939 saw the trustees prepare the chapel (Reheboth) for the war. Blackout curtains were purchased for the school and the side windows being covered in black paper. The gateposts and porch were painted white, and the school was offered to the government as an evacuation centre if required, Outwood then being more rural than it is today.

The school was not required, but a child welfare centre was opened on the premises in June 1940, with the school also being used as a Air Raid Patrol lecture theatre, with a charge of 3s 6d per lecture. The Girl Guides group and Brownies were formed the same year by Mrs Edna Chaplin and became the 18th Wakefield Girl Guide Company.

Margaret Walker,
writing about Reheboth Chapel, Victoria Corner, Outwood

Woodmoor Chapel, Newmillerdam, was opened in 1880 and closed in 1937. During the Second World War, the chapel, which had been empty for a number of years, was commandeered by the government and turned over to the local Home Guard Detachment. One of the lower vestries was fitted out as an armoury. The building was returned to the trustees of Lakeside Methodist Church, Newmillerdam in late 1945 and it was sold in the following year for £350, and was converted into a garage business. But in the mid-1980s, the building was restored and converted into four flats.

Margaret Firth

Wakefield Salutes the Soldier Week. General A.P. Shears addresses the assembled public from the Town Hall in Wood Street, 1944.

DUNKIRK

After Dunkirk Wakefield rapidly filled with battered wrecks of men, all highly nervous, and it was not advisable to come up behind them quietly. Pemberton House and Vincent House, on Westgate near the station, were full of men – often leaning from windows and calling out.

The Lupset estate, and certainly others, all had men billeted on them and the hospital blue pyjamas of the wounded men from Pinderfields became a common sight around the town. About 180 evacuees arrived from the Channel Islands and Miss Maris put them up in the Jubilee Hall, pending the finding of permanent homes. The only difficulty was, where would they go in case of an air raid or emergency?

Jeane Cresswell

Mrs Cresswell collected the names of many of these soldiers and rubbings of their cap badges in a pocket book. Some of the names recorded in the book are *A.L. Thomas*: 41st Battalion Royal Tank Regiment; *E.R. Griffiths*: 45th Battalion Royal Tank Regiment: 'A visitor from Birmingham' and *James C. Beech*: C Company, 1st Battalion East Yorks Regiment: 'a man from Hull'.

Mr and Mrs Ormison had a small grocery and news agency in Belle Vue, Wakefield. Troops rescued from Dunkirk were being camped in any available hall, and one afternoon an officer arrived at their shop. He had arranged sleeping accommodation for some of the troops billeted in the area, but had not been able to arrange to feed them, so could the Ormisons help. Mr Ormison went into town to a crockery shop for pint-pot mugs and to Hagenbachs, a wholesale bakery, for teacakes and buns. He called at the Conservative Club, behind St Catherine's church, where he was secretary, and obtained a bottle of rum from their stocks. Benches were arranged around the small shop, and then the lorry arrived with the men. Rum-laced tea, potted meat and fish paste sandwiches, and buns were on offer.

The troops were told not to worry about paying, but when the shop was emptied Mrs Ormison found coins tucked under jars, etc. She ran that canteen for several weeks while the troops were billeted nearby. Tea and a wad were ever ready for the men after doing drill on the nearby piece of ground. She kept her shop open late at night, so that those men who were not using the local pubs could come and have a tea while sitting and writing letters on paper and envelopes that she provided.

Ron Swinden

I lived with my mother and two brothers on the Lupset estate. I well remember Mr Fiske, the local police constable, come knocking at the door and telling my mother than she would have two soldiers billeted on her. This was odd as there was no man in the house. The elder of the soldiers, aged about fifty, was Mr Night, the younger, in his mid-twenties, was Mr Bacon. They stayed with us for about two weeks.

During the day, they met up with other soldiers at the Whinney Moor Public House, and they trained in the grounds and would clean their equipment – often Bren guns.

Our neighbours did not get soldiers billeted on them, and one wonders who chose which people the soldiers were to be billeted on. My mother was terrified of the men, but they were very kind and kept the lawns cut while they were with us.

Joyce Simpson

Deputy mayor Councillor H. Watson presents a member of Wakefield Army Cadet Corps with a proficiency certificate, 1943.

PC Fiske was our local copper, and if he had been in the police force for all his life, he would never have risen above the rank of constable.

When Dunkirk took place, trains had to be used to ferry thousands of troops from the south coast to holding camps further north. Railwaymen were called upon to work excessive hours to transport all those men from the beaches of Dunkirk. There were special Red Cross trains to transport those who were injured.

The southern railway men were the ones who bore the brunt of the work and worked for days without a break. They then handed the trains over to London North Eastern Railway and London Midland Scottish Railway to take the men to the hospitals and reception camps.

Railwaymen were the only workers who didn't receive danger money and were our unsung heroes during the Second World War. There was no organisation of the evacuated men and no order or system to it.

I thought it would have been better to try and group men by regiment rather than splitting them up all over the country. Trains pulled into Westgate and Kirkgate stations, and the men would be put into groups, and then distributed all over Wakefield by the police in Lupset.

Fiske or another copper would come round and knock on the door, and say that these men were billeted on you. We never had anyone billeted on us. It was a rather piecemeal affair.

Dennis Varey

A crashed gyrocopter on Low Hill. These primitive helicopters were developed in the 1920s and 1930s. The two views of the crash show the interest aroused by the crash as well as the unique free-spinning rotor blades above the cockpit.

BOMBING

After Dunkirk came the bombing of London, Birmingham, Coventry, Manchester and Liverpool and that unnamed east coast town – Hull – and of course the all-embracing south coast. Somewhere amongst this came Sheffield, when, for several hours for two nights, Wakefield citizens could see the reflection of the burning city in the sky, and could hear the bombers circling, and the local searchlights, one being at Snapethorpe school, quartered the sky looking for them. The skies would dull, the flashes of bombs exploding would be seen and the dull crump, crump, crump of the explosions heard and the sky flare up again.

Ruth Tetley

The night will remain forever in my memory. There had been several explosions quite nearby, shaking the house to its foundations. At that time I was attending the Wakefield School of Arts and Crafts, and on arriving the following morning, heard some devastating news. Mr Topping, one of our teachers, who lived on the opposite side of the park to me, had been on duty as an air raid warden. Before leaving home, he had instructed his wife and two small sons to remain in the shelter until he returned.

As there had been a lot of activity that night, he was unable to get back until well after the all clear had sounded. He was horrified on arriving home to see several houses on the opposite side of his street, razed to the ground, but relieved to see his own home intact. Rushing inside, he found a note from his wife. She had gone over the road to be with a friend. His entire family had been wiped out.

16 September 1940, it was around eight o'clock, on a beautiful evening, and looking up, we saw a plane. As we watched, something fell from it, making a peculiar whistling sound. Rushing back inside, we heard a huge explosion, whereupon I charged upstairs, grabbed my little sister who was asleep, and we all ran hell for leather to Mrs Hoole next door. There had been no air raid sirens. No warning whatsoever . . . Mam and Dad, hearing the explosion, which had shaken the house, downed tools immediately and raced home panic-stricken to see how we were. The bomb had landed at the entrance to the park, making a large crater, very close to the new house.

Following that incident, we had regular air raids, often having to sleep in the cellar. Several times the blast from nearby bombs blew the back door open, despite it having been securely locked.

Ruby Haggis

The chief designer of Drake & Warters, Hayden Suthill, was not frightened but terrified of being called up, and as he was an essential member of staff, Mr Drake moved heaven and earth to have him reserved. He was only to die some weeks later outside his own gate in the raid on Thrones Road on the night of Friday 4 March 1941: Wakefield's third and most devastating attack. The explosions killed five other people, ranging from a two-year-old child to an eighty-year-old man. Fifteen were injured, five seriously. Hayden Suthill was replaced by Pete Mundy. Fate is far more important than fear or planning.

Jeane Cresswell

I can still see the plane come in low, the bomb bay doors opening and this black object fall out. It fell somewhere near the recreation ground off Chantry Road, near to the quarry. As the bomb fell, we all rushed out of the house and into the Anderson shelter in the back garden Auntie Nelly Varey (née Harvey) and my mother, Clarice Hemingway (née Harvey), both tried to get into the shelter at the same time, which was quite impossible. The bomb turned out to be a dud, and it left a huge crater which meant we could not use the recreation ground until it had been cleared. There had been no air raid warning whatsoever.

Joyce Simpson (née Hemingway)

Bomb-damaged houses on Thornes Road.

When Belle Vue engine sheds were bombed, I remember sitting on top of our Anderson shelter watching the bombs drop. The shelters were very sturdy, made from corrugated steel, and sunk into the earth. Some of the shelters on Lupset were concreted in by the council, so they were dry. Not every house had one; I think it was a matter of choice. Some houses which did not have gardens, or the occupiers were elderly, had Morrison shelters. These were like a large metal box with a thick steel top, strong legs at each corner and mesh sides. One neighbour had hers in the front room and disguised it with a tablecloth. People who lived in the city centre terraces, with literally one or two rooms on each floor, in a back to back, either used the cupboard under the stairs, there being no cellar, or communal shelters.

Some Anderson shelters were built on land towards Snapethorpe Hospital off Gissing Road. Our Anderson shelter was very wet, but our neighbour's wasn't. You either died from pneumonia sitting in the shelter, had the possibility of drowning if a bomb landed nearby and you fell into the muddy water, or you took the risk and stayed indoors, or more often than not we went next door and used our neighbour's. The Anderson shelters made excellent garages after the war, and if you got hold of some more corrugated steel you could replace the centre section and make them about 9 feet wide.

Dennis Varey

THE BLACKOUT

The blackout, of course, affected everybody, and 'Turn that light out!' became a regular yell from air raid wardens. Fines were heavy for people not maintaining a strict blackout. This applied to cars whose headlamps had to be masked with just three slits on each light, and of course after 1940 all signposts, and in some cases street names, town boundary signs and anything that could give you an idea of where you were, were removed in case of invasion from the air. With only a torch covered with a mask to help you find your way about, life became difficult to say the least. 'Got your tin hat? Got your gasmask? Got your torch? Goodnight!' became a ritual saying and was heard virtually everywhere. In order to be able to identify your house, many people painted the door white, or the gateposts, so as to be visible at night.

Jeane Cresswell

RATIONING

In 1939 very few people were lucky enough to have a car and most travelled, and usually not very far, by either bus, tram or steam train (indeed some still travelled by horse, bus or pony and trap owing to the restrictions on petrol). The fuel for these became scarce as it was rationed. Mrs Tetley adds that: 'Bus windows were taped or netted to prevent flying glass and the lights were always very low, so much so one could not read the bus ticket.'

> The services were reduced and the buses very crowded. Private cars had a small, basic, allocation of petrol and eventually you had to prove your need for that. There were greater rations for essential work, but woe betide you if you were found outside your immediate area or latterly running on red petrol, which was regarded as a crime. Most cars were mothballed for the duration.
>
> Fuel of all sorts was valuable and every effort was made to save it. Coal was rationed, but gas – except for reduction of pressure – and electricity could not be, so in came the rule: if possible one bath a week, and only 5in of water. That did not mean 5in of boiling water to cool off with cold: 5in maximum. Many people measured a five-inch mark, and painted it on their baths. So 'Save Fuel, Save Lives' became a slogan. The war was full of slogans.
>
> *Ruth Tetley*

> Food of course was rationed and difficult to come by. All queued for everything from onions, fish, sausage, liver and even nylons. Anything that was not rationed had to be queued for. The smallness of rations did not affect everybody, as you ate what you were given. Fat ration was 4oz a week, as was sugar. Meat was 1s worth and you got half an egg a week. Some things like dried fruit, dried milk, dried eggs and certain tinned foods were on points. Each item was allocated a number of points and everybody was allocated so many a week, which could be used as you wished, always providing that anything was available, queues depending. Life was very difficult and very unfair for many. Anyone who had anything to exchange could usually have a barter system somewhere, and the black market was always there for anyone who had money. At and before the beginning of the war, people were encouraged to stock up on food as far as they could because shops could not carry very large stocks. Butter was preserved in crocks of saline solution, eggs in water glass, tinned

stuffs bought along with many other essentials. The older people who had been through the previous war were of course keener to do so than the 'war will be over by Christmas' people.

The real unfairness came when what had been a patriotic duty became regarded later as unfair and unpatriotic, and hoarding became almost criminal. It affected the middle class more than the working class, many of whom did not have the resources to stock up. 'Why should we go without when they have something' became a mindset for a lot of people.

The diet may have been restricted, but it was a healthy one – there were very few overweight children – and in some cases improved the diet of some families, and the children of the real poor were better fed than they would have been without the war, except in the cases, of which there were a number in Wakefield, where mothers sold their ration books.

Clothes were also rationed. Many servicemen came back to very reduced wardrobes where their trousers had been cut down for their sons or made into skirts for daughters. Jumpers were made from wool that had been unravelled from other jumpers then wound round pieces of card and steamed by the kettle until all the curl had gone out of it. The wool was then re-knitted. 'Make do and mend' was a slogan everyone knew. Fashion basically went out of the window as clothes were turned, many clothes were turned inside out and back to front and made up on the other side at least twice and of course the length then became shorter and shorter.

One of the features of the war years was the savings campaign when many saved money for themselves by buying War Savings Certificates, and at the same time helped to raise money for the war effort through their purchase. In 1942, Warship Week was held, only a few weeks after a previous Weapons Week. An ambitious target of £2,000 was set. An open day was held, where the minimum admission was a sixpenny savings stamp. On the stage was a model of a destroyer showing what total had been raised so far.

Evacuation was a big thing. Wakefield was lucky as it did not see the wholesale removal of children that London, Hull and other places saw. Nearby East Ardsley was a distribution centre for evacuees. The emotional stress and strain was colossal, but people were stronger, there was little moaning, and most weeping was done in private; people had their families close and supported each other.

Jeane Cresswell

5

War Work & After: Drake & Warters

D rake & Warters Ltd was one of the few Wakefield companies actively involved in sustaining the war effort. Other companies were involved, but they were not involved to the same extent as in the First World War, or to have done as much as Drake & Warters.

The toss of a coin between two managers at a small Wakefield joinery firm resulted in them starting up their own business – a company whose products were to be found in many towns and cities across the British Isles. The two men, Charles Henry Drake and Robert Warters, decided that if the coin fell heads up they would start a company. The coin duly landed with the monarch facing them, and the business of Drake & Warters Ltd, shopfitters and builders, was born.

The first headquarters of the company was a small wooden and corrugated iron shed and a converted railway carriage in Back Lane, behind the Playhouse cinema. The transport department consisted of a small handcart, with timber being carried from Westgate Station to the works. It was around this cart that the team spirit, for which the company was famed, was created. Everyone from directors to the office boy lent a hand when it came to fetching timber. As the business prospered it became harder and harder to push the cart up Back Lane. Mr Drake brought one of his ideas into use, and his belt-driven Scott motorcycle with sidecar was used to tow the handcart instead. Eventually, however, the handcart gave up the struggle and the wheels collapsed. That was the starting point for the works' purpose-built factory.

Responsibility fell into two sections. Charlie Drake was responsible for sales and outside supervision, while Mr Bob (Robert Warters) designed all the practical and manufacturing details. William Warters, Mr Bob's brother, took care of financial details on a part time basis until Mr Alexander was engaged full time.

In the early 1930s, most types of work were undertaken, including funeral directing.

Much work was done out of hours. Mr Bob would regularly bring plans and drawings of jobs back to his home for work in progress or new projects. After the evening meal he would clear the family's dining table and spread out his worksheets and clear out the family from the living room, which became the office. He would pore over the drawings until the early hours, doing costings. Charlie Drake would also be found most evenings measuring up shopfronts for new projects, organising timber, labour, and taking the costings to the client. During the day, No. 3, the works' sole lorry, would hurry out somewhere on a job, and in the evenings, many employees, including Charlie Drake, provided free labour to replace the materials used in that week's jobs.

Office accommodation at Thornhill Street was provided in the corner of the joinery factory run by Bill Warters, who was now a full time employee. Several men were now employed, many having joined from Judges – Fred Mundy, the first employee, George Kellet, Jack Beck, Mr Snowden, Joseph Tranter, Teddy Thresh, Alfred Batson, and many more including Irvine Bedford, Jack Nettleton, Billy Cole and Eric Petit.

Again the factory was extended many times to cope with increased capacity, until all available space was filled. Even an upper floor was provided over the loading bay yard to allow the lorries to be unloaded and loaded, and work go on overhead. This upstairs-downstairs existence continued for many years until larger premises could be purchased. During the 1930s, shopfitting was the only work undertaken, and that was all over the British Isles. Charlie Drake once remarked that there was not a single town or city in England, Ireland, Scotland, Wales, the Isle of Man or the Channel Islands where there was not some product of Drake & Warters. You could go into London's Regent Street, Leicester Square or the Strand and find Drake & Warters shopfronts and interior fittings. The firm fitted out some of the biggest firms in Leeds and Bradford. Many multiples were catered for, including Timothy Whites & Taylors, Boots, Maypole & Meadow, Homes and Colonial, Liptons, Schofields and many more.

So far as shopfitting was concerned, they were able to dismantle existing fittings, build a new shopfront or the whole building for that matter, and equip the interior in the space of the shop closing on a

/continued overleaf

/continued from previous page

Saturday evening and re-opening on the Monday at 9 a.m. The building side was carried out by Harry Hainsworth Ltd, which became Drake & Warters (Builders) Ltd in 1939, which in post-war years built many schools in the West Riding of Yorkshire, which Drake & Warters Ltd provided the internal fittings for. Drake & Warters supplied all the chairs and fitted out the science labs at Thornes House School, Wakefield in 1955/56.

On shopfitting jobs in the early days of the firm, everything that was needed from glass, woodwork, fittings and tools, was packed into a lorry, along with the employees and off they went, to return days later, proud of a job well done and that on a Monday morning, customers and employees would find a particular establishment with a completely new front and interior. Anyone who was left out of a job felt just about as happy as a player dropped from the cup team.

Most Fridays from 1938 found Charlie Drake in London on business. Here he was either meeting company directors for contracts for shopfittings or lobbying the Ministry of Works for contracts, as he believed war was going to happen. He would take the Yorkshire Pullman from Wakefield Westgate to Kings Cross. It was pulled by a streamlined locomotive and all the coaches were Pullmans.

Within weeks of war being declared, in a time known as the phoney war as there seemed to be no war at all, but the serious faces of my parents and people at chapel suggested otherwise, the company was building air raid shelters in Castleford, and a workman would not be seen by his family from Sunday to Sunday. Before this contract was complete, the building side of the company was busy starting to build army camps on green field sites at Hessle near Hull, and near Ripon in north Yorkshire. In order to prevent the docks at Hull being bombed a decoy port was created, which involved the digging of huge ditches and building light emplacements. Another decoy, this time a town, was built for Leeds, and consisted of roadways and large bonfire emplacements. Once the war started, Friday became Charlie Drake's usual day to go to the East Riding. In early days this was quite a trip, to visit the two camps that the company was building, pay wages and inspect development. As time went on other contracts saw the company build cubic tank traps, on the beaches between Flamborough Head, and Barmston Sands just south of Bridlington.

/continued on page 108

Charlie Drake outside the company's first headquarters, on Back Lane, riding his Rudge motorcycle.

/continued from page 106

The party would collect the liaison officer, usually a captain, in Beverly and would pass through the sentry posts, and so paddled in the sea and saw mines being laid on the beaches, and walked along cliffs, between the ever present danger of minefields and witnessed gun emplacements being constructed. The works also built an army camp at Hessle near Hull, and a huge drain was dug at Tranby. Several searchlight emplacements were built near Ripon and in the Wakefield area – one was at Snapethorpe Hall – and concrete tank traps and gun emplacements were built on the north-east coast. Surprisingly, beach material could not be used in the concrete, so river sand and gravels had to brought on to the sites.

Jeane Cresswell

Charlie Drake and Robert Warters in the entrance to the company's offices, 1924. This was a converted railway wagon.

Whitby, 1942. At this time Drake & Warters were involved in building anti-tank traps and gun emplacements all along the east coast.

Bomb-damaged Sheffield, which Drake & Warters helped to rebuild.

Employees of Drake & Warters enjoying a break, c. 1930.

The decoy port mentioned by Jeane Cresswell on p. 106 was an exact copy of Hull docks but built further inland, complete with floodlights, to deceive the German bombers. It was the subject of a BBC 2 programme as part of the *Time Fliers* series. All this work has gone unrecorded in Wakefield's history, and is largely forgotten.

In later days, when the real war had started, many hours were spent in bomb-damaged Beverley Barracks watching the troops training. Mrs Cresswell clearly remembers her and her father having to run for their lives, along with the liaison captain, when the street that they were on was strafed with machine-gun fire.

These trips to north Yorkshire did not last as long, but were equally exciting, mainly because of the great desire of the dispatch riders, who guided the party about in the area, to lose the party somewhere – they never managed but the party would never have found the camps without them.

Another of the company's interests at the time was the production and selling of anti-blast devices to stay shop windows. They were like spiders which were held in the centre of each side of the glass and stayed with wires to each corner, and were supposed to damp the ripples and vibrations that would be set up in the glass by an explosion.

Slowly of course these physical preparations were completed and the builders become occupied with repairing bomb damage to civilian and military buildings, and the factory turned from making army huts to the fittings for them, namely chairs, bunks, and bedside cabinets.

Work was also found for the factory, and large contracts were obtained from the Ministry of Defence for thousands of wardrobes and folding chairs for the RAF – innovative designs by Mr Warters – and bedside cabinets and officers' camp beds. 250,000 bunk beds were also made for the American army, and the construction of thousands of work benches and cupboards to equip shadow factories, such as those for Rover.

Jeane Cresswell

D-DAY PREPARATIONS

The build up to D-Day changed the lives of all the families involved with Drake & Warters. In 1943, Charlie Drake had obtained a contract to build sixteen landing craft assault (LCA) vehicles. This requirement was later expanded to seventy-two units. In order to fulfil this contract a quick expansion of the labour force was required and 800 girls were taken on. The Navy christened the company the boat builders of Back Street. So unusual was this development that BBC Radio interviewed Charlie Drake and made a newsreel for broadcasting to the nation. Drake's nephew by marriage, Eric Bradley, saw the film as a captain on the staff in Bombay. The small boats built by Drake & Warters were used on D-Day to transport soldiers from large troop ships to the beaches.

They were simple, flat-bottomed craft with armour, 43ft long with a 10ft 6in beam, and weighed 12½ tons. The engines fitted to the original sixteen LCAs were conversions of motorcar engines. Harry Warters carried out the fittings, often using Ford V-8s. They were built on specially produced jigs in the factory. Owing to the shortage of teak and plywood, mahogany was used. Wearing their grey overalls, and forged into a team by Bob Warters, the girls could be found tapping screws. They not only planked the hull and built the frames, but they also made the internal fittings and oil and water coolers. Female electricians made the instrument boards and switch panels. The highly skilled girls worked on the sheet metalling as well, adapting aero engines to marine use. The female workers' duties also included the hammering of thousands of rivets and the tightening of hundreds of nuts and bolts to give the craft the necessary strength. They also manufactured and bolted on the armour plate, assisted in the installation of engines and gave the craft its final coat of grey paint. The structure had two half decks to afford the infantry on board protection during an assault and had plate armour capable of deterring a machine-gun bullet. The later LCAs were fitted with two purpose-built Austin engines that were capable of developing 390hp each. Fully laden with fifty troops, and equipped with machine guns and mortars, the craft had a draught of less than 2ft with the propellers shielded in shallow tunnels to prevent damage upon landing.

The preferred age of the women workers was between fifteen and thirty. The number of educated women working in the factory was noticeable; but skill, the experienced foreman would tell you, had nothing to do with education. The vast majority of the girls had never worked before and those who had had generally come from offices where they worked as typists or receptionists – scarcely a grounding for a life of manual labour.

One great advance made in the production of the craft was the establishment of a central logistics unit, albeit only in 1944. It was the role of this unit to establish the requirements of all the small factories and ensure that the required material would be delivered to the right place at the right time. Central stores were set up, and daily lorries or the railway collected the next portions of the craft required. You could have an LCA delivered to the factory in pieces, like a giant jigsaw in its component parts. The first LCAs were made from scratch, with only the aid of diagrams, blueprints and input from a Mr Lehman, who was appointed to assist in their construction by the Ministry of Defence.

A novel aspect of the contract was the fact that Wakefield was, and still is, land locked; the factory was a mile from the nearest waterway. Once finished, an LCA was rolled out of the works' main entrance, and a special frame was erected to load it on to the back of a lowloader – nicknamed the Queen Mary. It was then taken by road to Earnshaw's timber yard in Doncaster Road, a distance of nearly a mile, where a dock had been excavated. The craft was then launched into the canal to run trials; a system controlled by Naval officers and the Ministry. The first trip was several miles along the Calder & Hebel navigation, through a series of locks, to the River Aire at Knottingley. Here, in the presence of Naval experts, the craft had to pass tests on a measured mile and prove that it was capable of achieving the required speed. Few naval craft have such a peculiar start to life as these assault craft built in Yorkshire. The Naval officers present at the tests were inevitably Lieutenant Charles Warren and Sub-Lieutenant Geoffrey Canadine.

The first LCA, number 1144, was launched on 13 October 1943. It was a thrilling day for the employees of Drake & Warters, and the citizens of Wakefield who flocked to see Wakefield's war effort. The first craft took six weeks and four days to build from the laying of the keel. By the time of the first launch seven other craft were on the stocks in various stages of construction, and, by 1944, there was a launch of a newly completed craft every week.

The 'Queen Mary' with the first LCA, which is about to be launched at Earnshaw's timber yard, 13 October 1943.

Mrs C.H. Drake launches the LCA, October 1943.

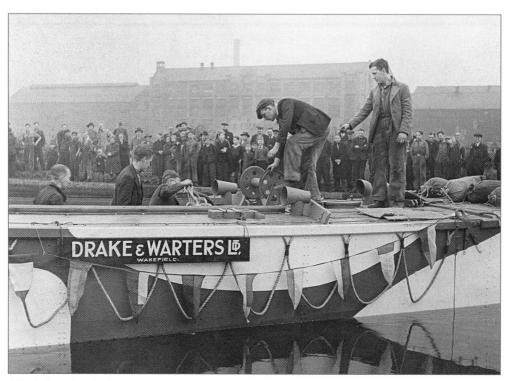

The LCA after its launch.

Wakefield citizens stand before the 'Queen Mary' to be photographed with Wakefield's war effort.

Present at the launch were Wakefield sea cadets. Here they are being inspected.

At the same event, Mrs C.H. Drake presented the Drake & Warters proficiency cup to the sea cadets.

The presentation of the cup.

POSTWAR

After the war, reconstruction of war-damaged Britain became the staple work of Drake & Warters. Housing had become an urgent priority; the incoming Labour government announced the building of 400,000 prefabricated houses. Drake & Waters obtained a large proportion of the contract. In total, 178,000 prefabricated wooden houses were shipped to Dumbarton, on the back of lorries, twice a week. In addition to this, by 1950 a further 16,800 prefabricated houses had been shipped to other towns in Scotland and 8,000 housing units for Glasgow alone. In total, just over half the total number of house shells ordered by the government had been supplied by Drake & Warters. As well as building prefabricated houses, by 1950 3,000 brick dwellings had also been built in both Wakefield and Scotland.

There had been a number of changes in the buildings, as the fleet of vehicles used by the company increased; twenty-two vehicles are listed in 1949. A garage and motive power depot was established on Ings Road. This repaired both the company's vehicles and undertook private repairs.

Storage also became difficult, and land was rented, in the cattle market off George Street, to store air-dry timber. Holdsworth the tailors on the corner of Thornhill Street and Charlotte Street was purchased in about 1948, and the house was turned into staff flats. The shop, workroom and storage space were converted into the painting and decorating department. The land between Charlotte Street and Grove Road was purchased as a plywood store and an area for the spraying of motor vehicles. Charlie Trantor was the paint shop manager in the 1950s, Sidney Moss the layout foreman and Jim Powell the assistant secretary.

Labour was short and directed in the immediate postwar years, so several houses were purchased to house Italian workmen. The houses were 46–52 Grove Road, bought for £1,300; Flats 41 and 41a Charlotte Street, for £1,100; 61 and 63 Ings Road, for £720; 39 Charlotte Street, for £400; 25, 25a, 27 and 27a Thornhill Street, for £120, 63 Ings Road, for £900; and Holdsworth House, Thornhill Street, for £1,400.

The company celebrated its Silver Jubilee in 1949/50. A celebratory dinner was held in Unity Hall, Wakefield, when the oldest employees – Fred Mundy, Ernest Blakey, George Kellit, Joseph Tranter, John Beck and Edwin Thresh – were presented with silver tankards, inscribed with the recipient's name and the words 'In appreciation of a workman and a friend of 25 years standing'. Charlie Drake and Mr Bob also exchanged tankards and the employees presented both men with silver candlesticks.

When the Yorkshire Show visited Wakefield on 26–29 July 1949, Drake & Warters built a large stand. The display took full marks for originality, style and effect with the tall steel scaffolding and dummy workman silhouetted against the sky. This was the first time the firm had exhibited at a show on their own account, and they were pleased with their success and surprised by the number of enquiries received about future contracts. This led the company to build the show stand for British Jeffrey Diamond at the British Industrial Fair held in Birmingham in 1950.

The machines installed in the factory made it possible for rough planks to be brought in, put through various processes and machines and turned out as high grade furniture or shop fittings. The fact that freshly hewn timber could be taken into the factory and turned out three weeks later in the shape of furniture was due to the use of a drying kiln, which was the only one in the north of England at the time. Seven hundred cubic feet of timber could be stacked in the kiln, and the workers at the control board studied dials and graphs and operated valves, to keep correct temperatures. The difficult part of the job was to keep the moisture content of the kiln at the same level as that in the outside layers. Great care had to be taken when the timber was removed from the kiln, especially if the day was wet or the atmosphere damp.

Inside the main shop were saws that could cut through oak boards faster than a warm knife through butter. A double-ended tenon machine, one of the most modern in the world, could produce 2,000 tenons a day. A man working with hand tools could average about twenty a day. There was little in the line of woodworking that it could not do. Nearby was an electric router, which operated at anything from 18 to 24,000 revolutions a minute. In fact, Charlie Drake once boasted that the electrical supply to the factory had to be stepped up to give direct drive to this machine, which took five minutes to slow down when the brake was not used. With this machine it was possible to cut out a person's name, in wood, in almost the exact handwriting of the writer, except at a larger scale. There was also a machine that collected all the sawdust and compressed it together with glue to make hardboard.

Bernard Hartley

The new factory was completed by 1939, and included the boardroom, which was described as the nearest thing that Wakefield had to a top flight Hollywood executive's office, seen in films of the period. The walls were panelled with mahogany and advaporie, an obscure West African wood selected for its finish by Bob Warters. In the centre of the room stood the boardroom table, with a finish that would have taken the breath away of most housewives. Mounted on the wall was the coin that Messrs Drake & Warters used as a decider. The coin, a penny, was minted in 1920.

Shopfitting and repair work was beginning to come back as time went on in the late 1940s. Another unusual and interesting order was for twelve speedboats. These boats were fitted with twin Austin Healy engines, and were built in similar jigs used for the LCAs. However, they were too fast for British waters, and were shipped to Barbados. They were dispatched to the Caribbean on a cargo ship, and were to appear at the New York Boat Show. The cargo ship was late on arrival, and the speedboats were never to appear at the boatshow, much to the detriment of Drake & Warters.

Bank fittings, school fittings and museum fittings helped to keep the machines busy. The paint shop was kept busy in 1947 when they re-gilded both the weathercock from the cathedral spire, which is only 2 feet 11 inches tall, and the rood screen figures. As well as this, set designs were made for the Little Theatre, Queen Street, housed in the former Market Street Primitive Methodist church. Due to the hard work of Charlie Drake, the building division was sub-contracted by the National Coal Board to build pit head baths at many of the local pits, such as Sharlestone Main and Low Ackworth. The work was often inspected every Sunday, during an afternoon drive in his Austin limousine.

Jeane Cresswell

The cattle market site was given up in 1952/3 and land in Tadmen Street, Thornes, was purchased. Robert Warters' son, Laurence, was taken into the firm in the late 1940s and Rex Boutland Cresswell, Charlie Drake's son-in-law, was taken into the shopfitting side in 1950 in an effort to provide continuity. Mr Cresswell was taken in initially as travelling sales representative, and learnt his trade through close supervision. His first installation as site supervisor was Ann's Pantry in Dewsbury. Others that followed included Page Fashions, Northgate, Wakefield. He worked through all the departments and eventually became company secretary. For the coronation of Queen Elizabeth II, the company, under the guiding hand of Mr Cresswell, made all the decorations for Pontefract and Castleford. For the information of any interested statisticians, the 2 miles of red, white and blue waxed paper used for Pontefract weighed just less than 2 tons, and cost £528. It was, however, the length and weight, rather than the cost, which concerned Mr Cresswell. It was a bright idea that solved the problem of how to transport the garlands. Mr Cresswell used the 22ft long trailer, used by the firm to carry long articles used in shop fitting. He fitted 5ft high sides to it, and found that it just contained a mile of garland, carefully folded lengthwise along the trailer. The garlands were hung in Beast Fair Pontefract and Carlton Street Castleford.

Charles Henry Drake and Robert Warters, presenting each other with tankards, at the company's Silver Jubilee in 1949/1950.

The 1950s were a period of great optimism. Shopfitting continuing to be the main source of income, though the production of manufactured joinery declined. New railway engine sheds were constructed at Wakefield Westgate station, and at the Belle Vue Motive Power Depot. New office blocks and banks were built and fitted out. Experiments were also made at producing flat-packed furniture at this time. Tenders were submitted for providing the fittings for the new development at Primrose Hill, Wakefield. The firm also supplied new fittings for the shop of Double Two and the Empire cinema.

The painting and decorating department's handiwork was to be seen in many of Wakefield's new homes, churches, chapels and business. It even repainted an Edwardian carousel, for the Heath Common fair, which over-wintered in Wakefield, and provided theatre scenes for the recently opened Little Theatre on Market Street. With the death of Charlie Drake, at the end of January 1964, the company continued under the direction of Robert Warters, with input from the likes of Joe Tranter, Percy Firth, Jack Nettleton and several others. During this time the Tadmen Street land was sold off and the transport department reduced. The company slowly started to modernise as the 1960s advanced, through the efforts of Mr Cresswell and others, and in 1967, the company purchased a Sterling Anita Mark 10, which was marketed as the 'world's first electronic desk computer in sterling mode' and

Staff were promoted from within; no outside brains were brought in. In-house apprentices became outside salesmen and representatives, and slowly became in charge of the practical side of things. This, whilst a very good thing at first, eventually meant that the company became more and more isolated from the mainstream of thought and old fashioned, and the main movers growing older. This became very obvious with the decline in health of Charlie Drake at the end of 1960 and thoughts turned toward the future, and a sale was beginning to be negotiated with Associated Dairies, now ASDA, and Carlton Holdings during 1962. However, ASDA wanted to buy not only Drake & Warters, but also Mr Drake, who they and many in the outside world saw as Drake & Warters personified. Charlie Drake was the company's front man, managing director and chairman, and a natural sales man. He was a dynamic personality, who, it was said, radiated modern ideas. Both Mr Bob and Charlie Drake needed each other, and were the very essence of a successful partnership. However, Charlie Drake courted the limelight, and was seen by the shopfitting and manufactured joinery world as the face of Drake & Warters. Neither Mr Bob nor his wife Florence were comfortable in the glow of the spotlight, and Florence in particular hated the big occasion. Mr Warters was well regarded among the small businessmen around Wakefield from where much of the company's early work and profits emanated. Both men were looked upon as 'Mr Drake & Warters' by different and equally important circles. Mr Warters, the secretary, was a member of the Wakefield Cricket, Bowling and Athletic Club, a keen gardener, and is recorded at the Jubilee Dinner, by the *Wakefield Times* of March 1950, saying that 'he left all the running around and organisation to Mr Drake'.

June Vaughan

'the most powerful and versatile desk top calculating medium available to British management today'. Drake & Warters was the first company in the Wakefield area to use computers. Many new buildings were built in Wakefield in the 1960s and 1970s, including the new shopping arcade around the Bull Ring, Little West Gate, Westgate and Silver Street on the site of the church institute.

The company continued in profit until the sudden death, in May 1974, of Mr Warters. Alexander & Sagar and Weatherhall, Hollis & Gate, in December of that year, proposed a sale to Simon's of Leicester, which was then a very big company. However, owing to the market conditions, the sale fell through.

Laying the foundation stone of Huddersfield Co-operative Stores, 1952.

When the company went into receivership, in August 1975, the full reasons were unclear. The board of directors at this time consisted of J. Warters, Jack Cooke (Charlie Drake's half-brother), Mrs S. Murdock (née Drake), D. Blakeaway, J. Powell, T.P. Scott, J. Nettleton and R. Brook. The fixtures and fittings were sold at auction on Tuesday 11 and Monday 17 November 1975, and raised the sum of £32,343.84. In the spring of the following year the land and buildings were sold to the Anchor Housing Group for £85,000. Many believed that if Anchor could build houses on the site, it was not beyond the realms of possibility that Drake & Warters would have been able to. They were, after all, builders.

Writing in the *Wakefield Times* of 31 March 1950, Charlie Drake had commented, accurately, that when it came to changing the face of Wakefield, it would be quite safe to say that the firm of Drake & Warters had led the field.

6

Victory & Into the 1950s

Victory in 1945 heralded a new wave of optimism. But the war had left Wakefield a long lasting and valuable legacy in the shape of Pinderfields hospital. The hospital had been designated, during the war, as an emergency hospital and accommodation for evacuees from Hull and London. It had received the first casualties on February 18 1940 and became part of the National Health Service in 1948 along with Stanley Road Hospital, forming Wakefield [B] Group Management Committee. Walton Hall maternity hospital, Manygates maternity hospital, Clayton hospital, the County General hospital, Oulton Hall, Cardigan sanatorium, Snapethorpe isolation hospital, Carr Gate hospital and Hatfield Hall became Wakefield [A] Group Hospital Management Committee.

The population growth, along with the raising of the school leaving age through the Butler Education Act of 1944 and 1947, put heavy pressure on existing schools, so the council embarked on scheme to provide new buildings and establishments. The growth of educational opportunities was matched by the increasing popularity of television, which quickly began to replace more traditional forms of entertainment. Improvements in technology and general economic buoyancy soon meant that the television became an affordable luxury, which heralded a decline in attendances at the city's cinemas and sole remaining theatre. The Theatre Royal and Opera House closed in 1954 and re-opened the following year as the Essolo cinema. Wakefield was not to have another theatre for a period of seven years, when the Little Theatre opened in the former Market Street Methodist church. In 1955 the Carlton cinema, on Grove Road, closed its doors for the final time, followed by the Rex cinema on Stanley Road and the Savoy cinema in Middlestown in 1959.

Wakefield rugby had been thrust on to the national stage when David Storey's first novel, *This Sporting Life*, was published. When, on 11 March 1963, a gala performance of the film adaptation was hosted at the Picture House, it was a boost to Wakefield cinematic life. The film starred the internationally renowned Richard Harris. Some of the scenes were shot at Wakefield Trinity's Belle Vue ground, and after the film, stars Jack Watson and Anne Cunningham were treated to a civic reception on the circle foyer. The book later went on to win the Macmillan Fiction Award.

The same year saw Wakefield Trinity winning the Rugby League Challenge Cup. The team brought the trophy with them when they attended a matinee before an enthusiastic audience, at the Regal/ABC on Kirkgate, of a newsreel of the team's victory at Wembley Stadium.

The VE Day celebratory dinner in the Unity Hall.

Field-Marshal Bernard Montgomery inspects the King's Own Yorkshire Light Infantry.

On the same day, Monty was given the Freedom of the City of Wakefield.

On 4 January 1947, Wakefield Trinity played Wigan at Belle Vue in the cup final. Wakefield Trinity won the game. The players from left to right are, back row: Baddeley, Higgins, Exley, Longley, Marson, Booth, Howes, Blan, Bratley, Atkinson, Shovaton, Ratcliffe, Lawrenson, Banks, Ward, Woosey; front row: Brooks, Banks, Perry, Stott, Wilkinson, Teall, Cunliffe, Mountford, Toohey, Nordgren.

Drake & Warters award-winning stand at the 1949 Great Yorkshire Show.

D-DAY ONWARDS

On June 6 1944 came D-Day. It was not a particularly happy day as a good friend was dropped with other paratroopers into Caen. He was home wounded within a week. Then on it went, pins marching across Europe again, but this time advancing. Then came Ravensbrück, Bergen-Belsen, days when the newspapers, and more so the newsreels at the cinemas – the Savoy on Horbury Road, the Regal, Grand Electric to name a few – made life unbearable and catastrophic for many. Then of course came VE Day, and the people of Wakefield celebrated in Wood Street outside the Town Hall. At school, we assembled at the usual time in the morning, but after assembly there was a ceremony when the flag was raised on the lawn and the whole school marched down to the cathedral for a joint service of thanksgiving with the boys from Queen Elizabeth Grammar School, conducted by the provost.

This war had been very different from the First World War; there were no serried trenches, there were few artillery barrages as such, except El Alamein. After El Alamein it was Tunis, Sicily, Normandy, the Rhine. Monty became a real hero of the people, and was given the Freedom of the City of Wakefield in 1947. People turned out in their hundreds to see and cheer their hero – the Cromwell with the common touch. He stayed in Wakefield with his batman, Sir Richard O'Brien, a native of Wakefield, who attended Holy Trinity church on George Street. O'Brien resided on South Parade, his neighbour being the mayor of Wakefield at the time, Harry Watson, who had invited Monty to visit the city. The same year the Queen visited Wakefield and two years later Princess Elizabeth and the Duke of Edinburgh visited the Great Yorkshire Show.

Gradually things at school began to return to normal, not to 1939, as many thought would happen. With the end of the war, Wakefield was a very different place to that of 1939. Bomb-damaged houses on Belle Vue and Thornes Road were replaced, so much so that you cannot tell that they were ever destroyed. The council embarked on a great rebuilding of the city. Slums were cleared, roads widened with a general feeling of optimism for the future. In 1949 the Great Yorkshire Show came to Wakefield. The three-day show had not been here since 1870 and demanded all the organisational skill the corporation and local business could muster.

Jeane Cresswell

As Wakefield entered the late 1950s the corporation embarked on an unprecedented number of building projects. This was the era of bigger is better, and the city got its first high rise blocks of flats. The coming of supermarkets in the 1960s did away with the more traditional way of shopping, though a new market house was built in 1964 replacing its Victorian predecessor. The new market hall cost near £300,000 and contained approximately ninety stalls, with the fish and meat stalls being housed in the Victorian meat market buildings nearby.

In the 1960s the land next to Wesley Hall Methodist chapel became Empire Stores, and of course, due to the increase in the number of cars and the M1 being built, there was a gradual decline in the standard and efficiency of public transport. Railway lines were closed, the clock tower of Westgate station being a victim of modernisation when the then rather run-down Victorian station was replaced with the current structure.

Shirley Murdock

Wakefield city council's proposed plans for Primrose Hill. Homes fit for heroes had been promised after the First World War, and again after the Second. As far back as 1888, leading citizens of Wakefield had argued that Primrose Hill was in need of redevelopment, to replace the run down and overcrowded terraced housing that had been built in the 1860s. Nothing was done until the 1950s. The Revd H.G. Parrish of St Mary's church, Primrose Hill, was just one of a number of late Victorian social commentators in Wakefield who saw the need to build better and cleaner housing for the poor and working classes.

A new Wakefield was built in the 1950s and 1960s. The stark concrete and glass is in stark contrast to the older, more mellow Georgian and Victorian houses and shops. M&S opened a new shop in Upper Kirkgate where it remains to this day. Lipton's had a superior shop in the new Bull Ring, as did Timothy Whites & Taylors. The new Bull Ring did not include the statue of Queen Victoria who was moved to Clarence Park, but has been returned to where she was intended to stand. It is this new Wakefield that will be familiar to the reader, which is already making way for an even newer 'new Wakefield'.

Ruth Tetley